INSPIRATIONAL FRACTALS

BY MARY KEI

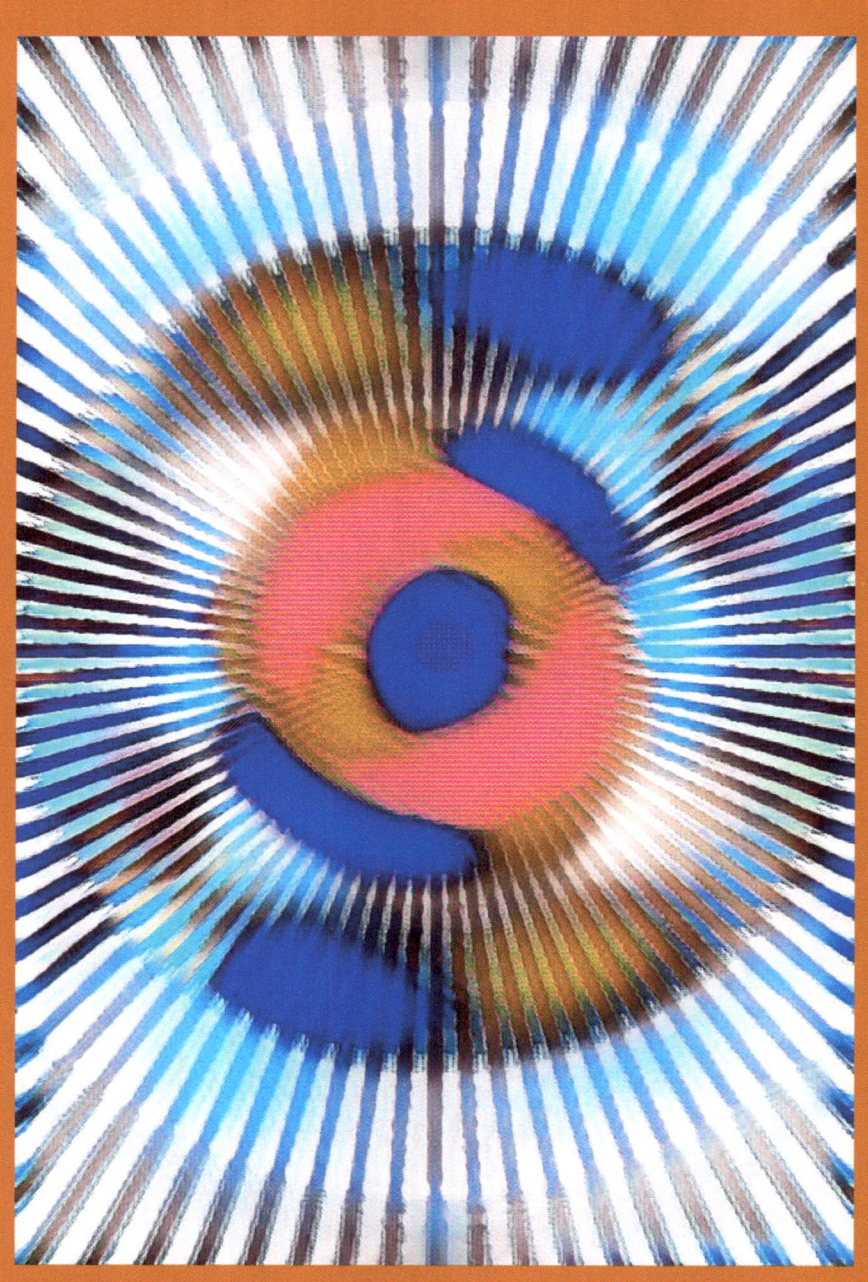

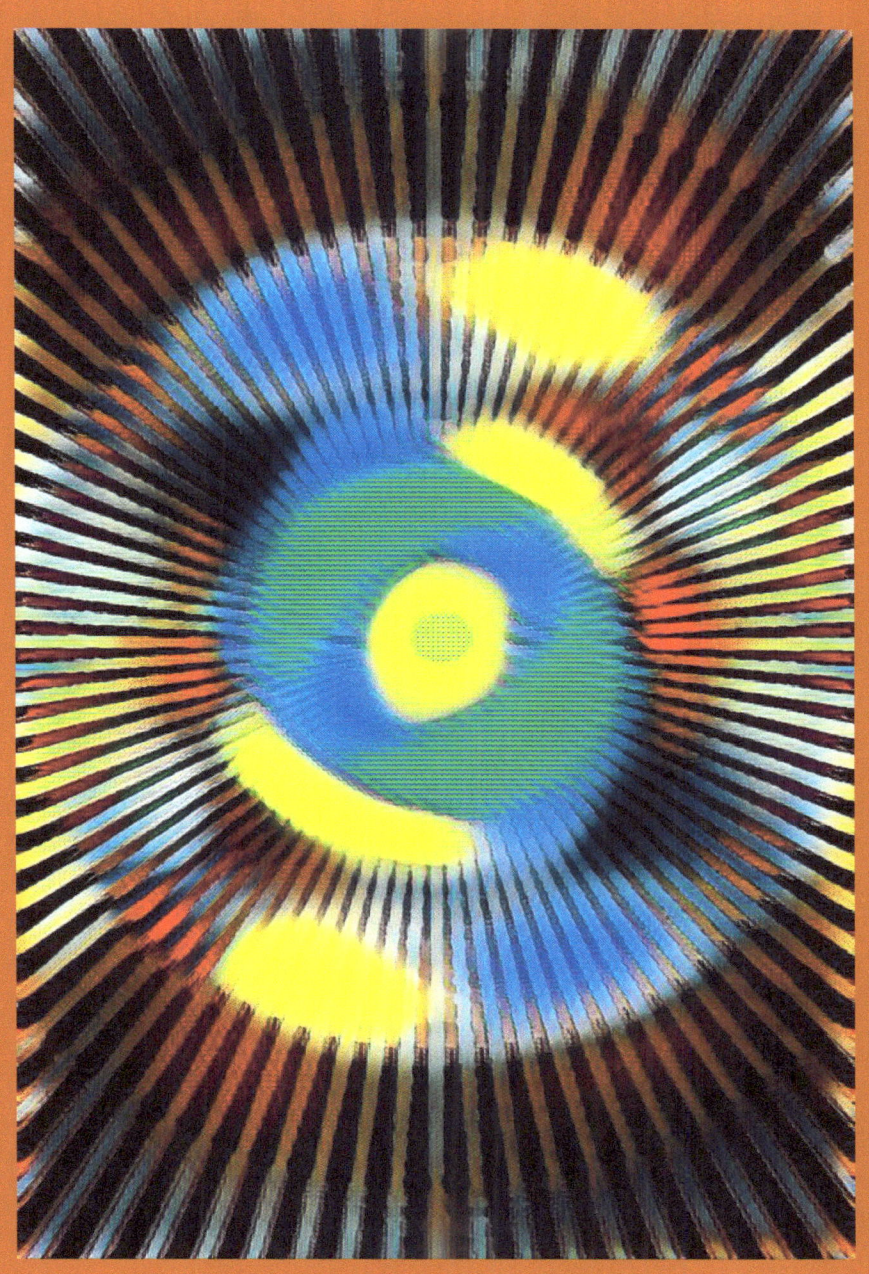

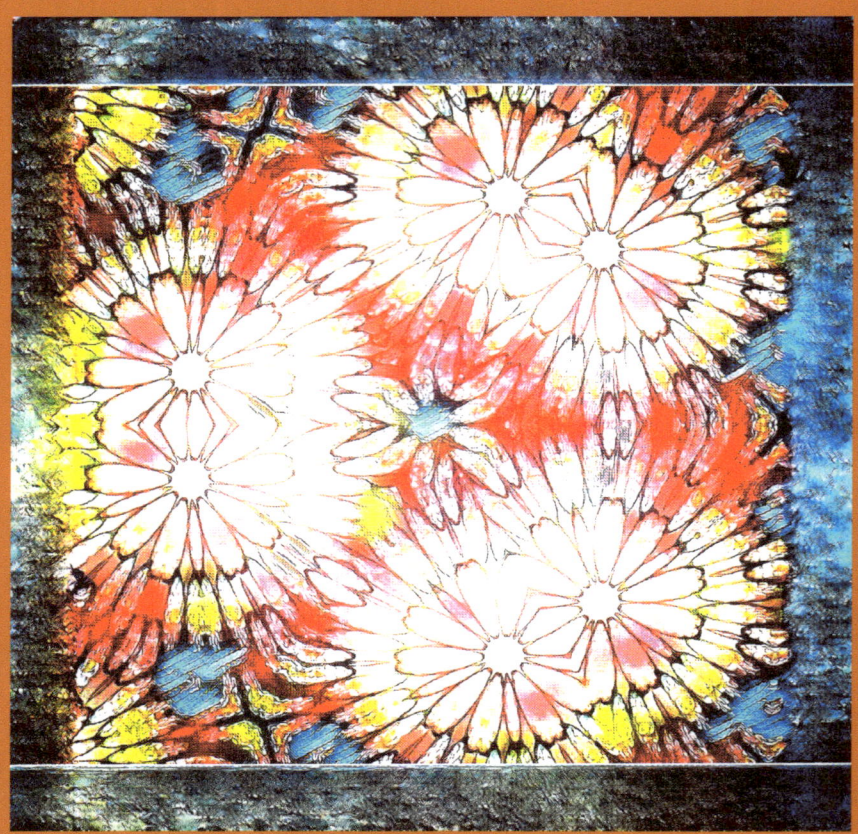

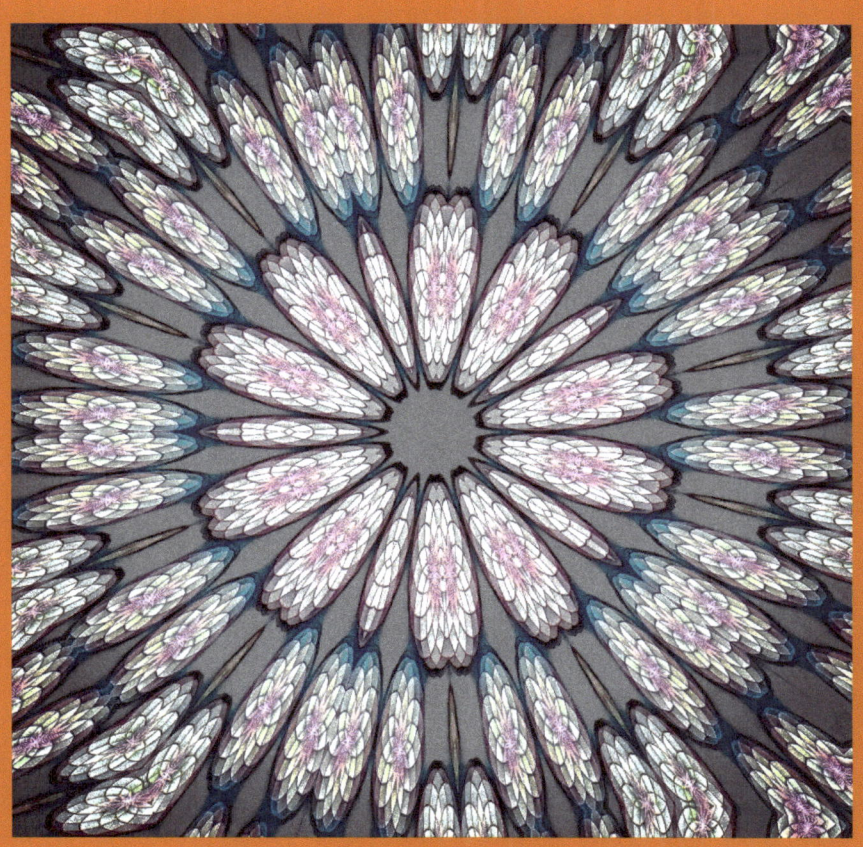

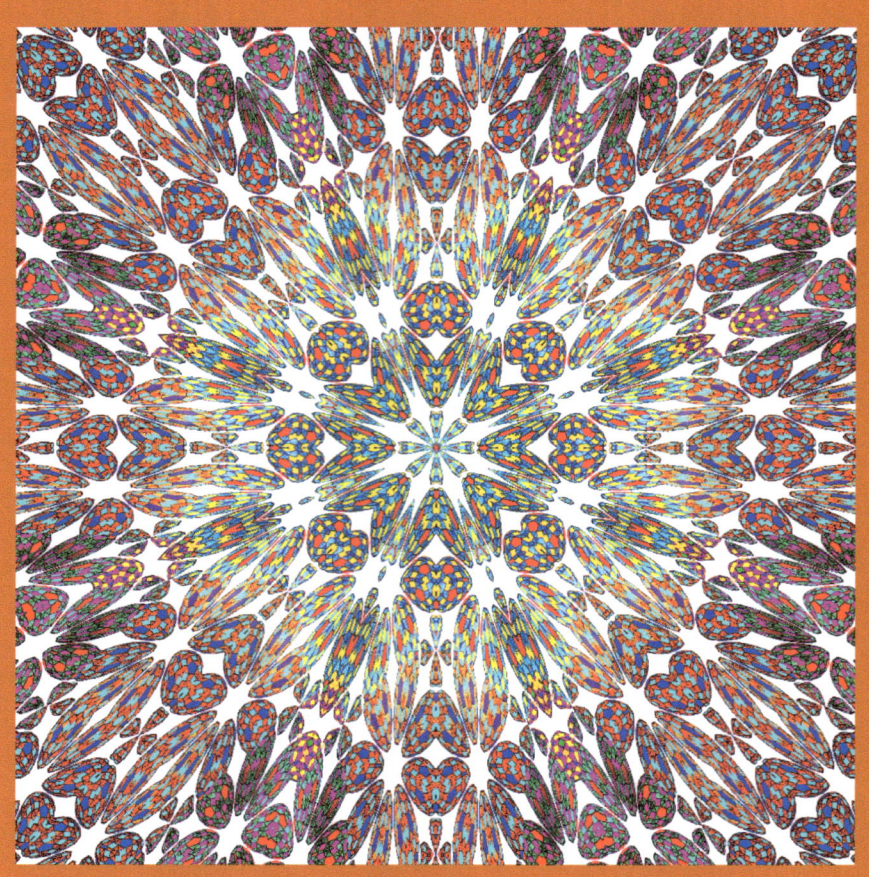

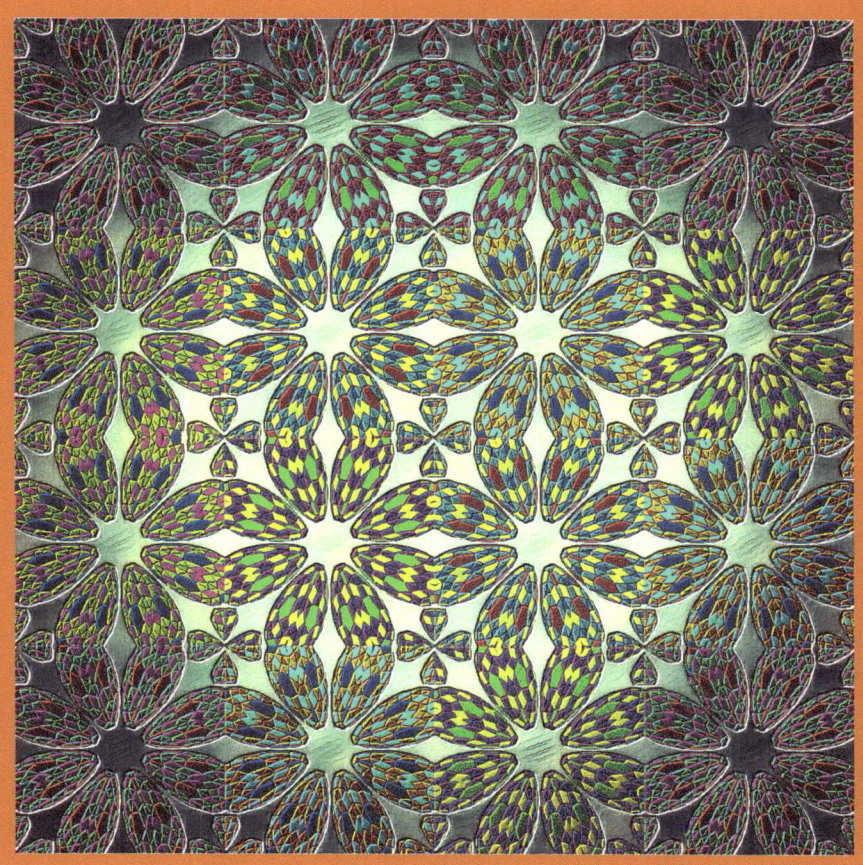

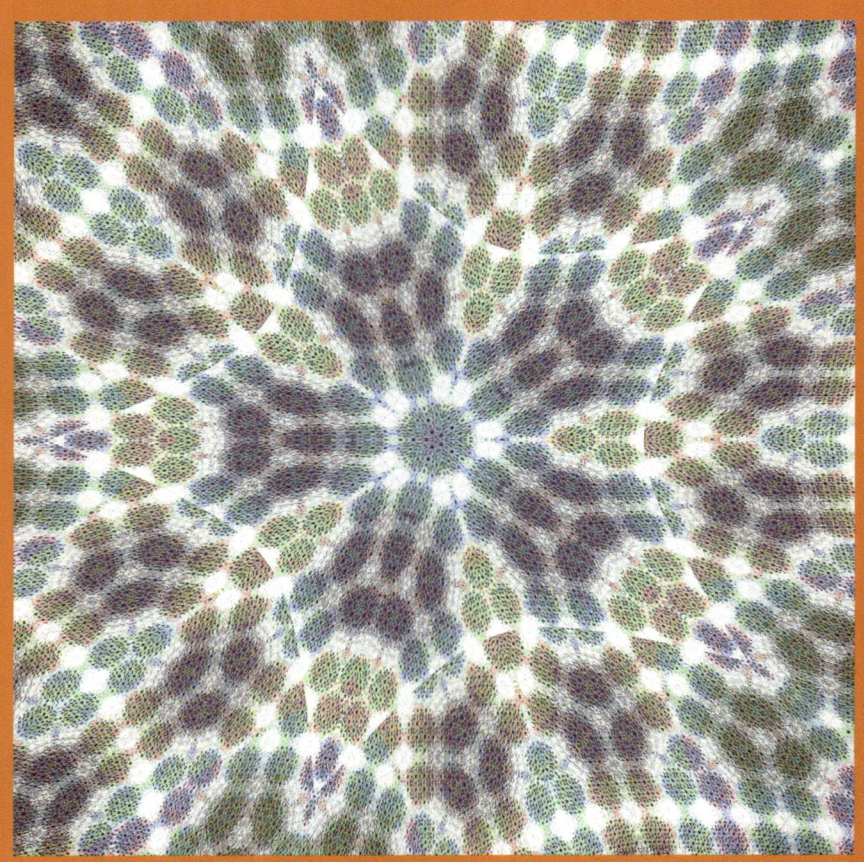

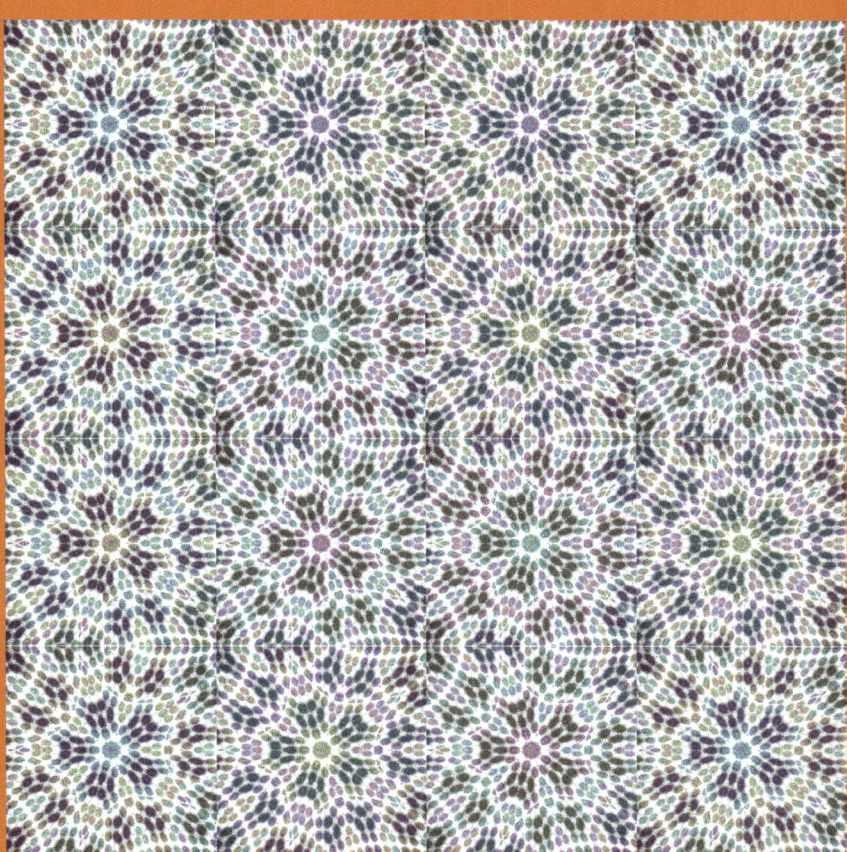

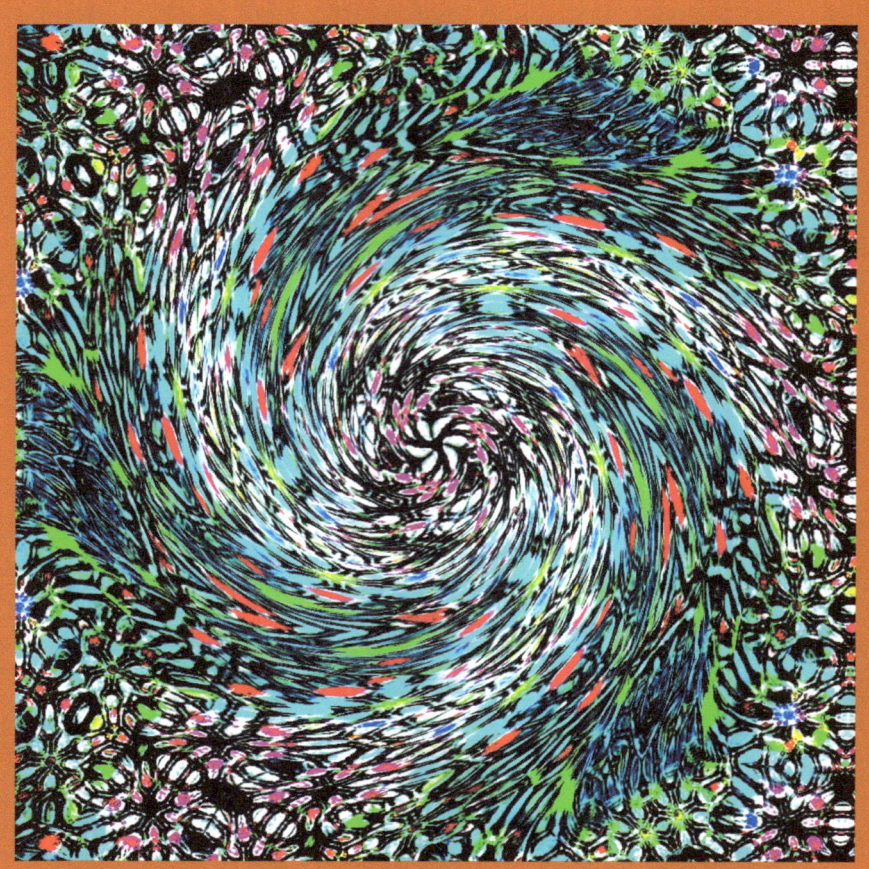

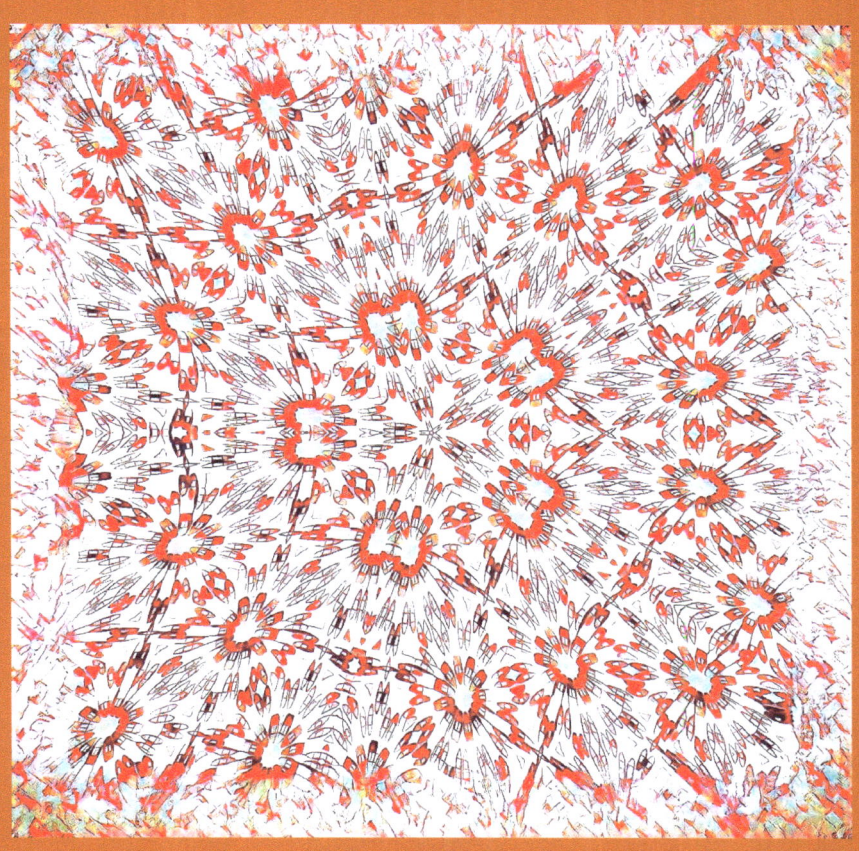

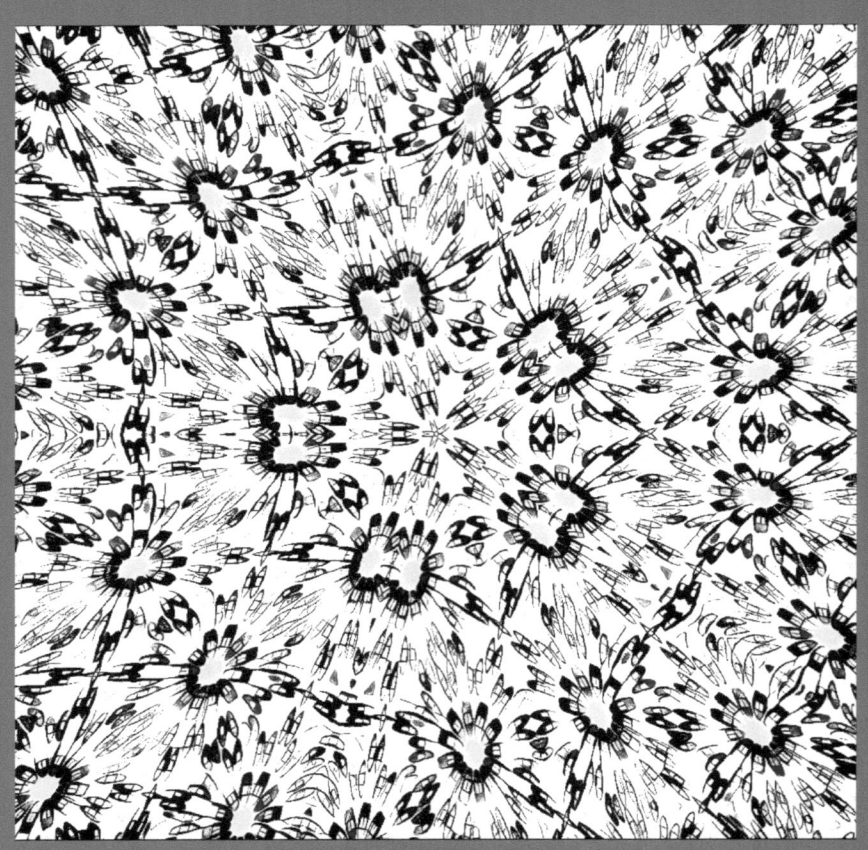

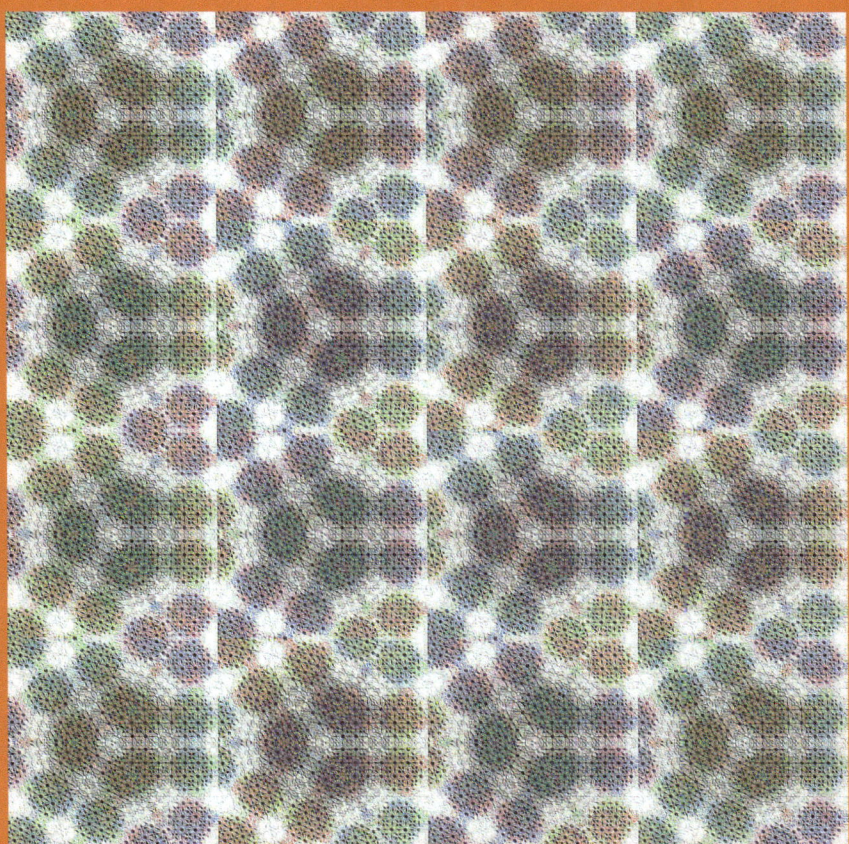

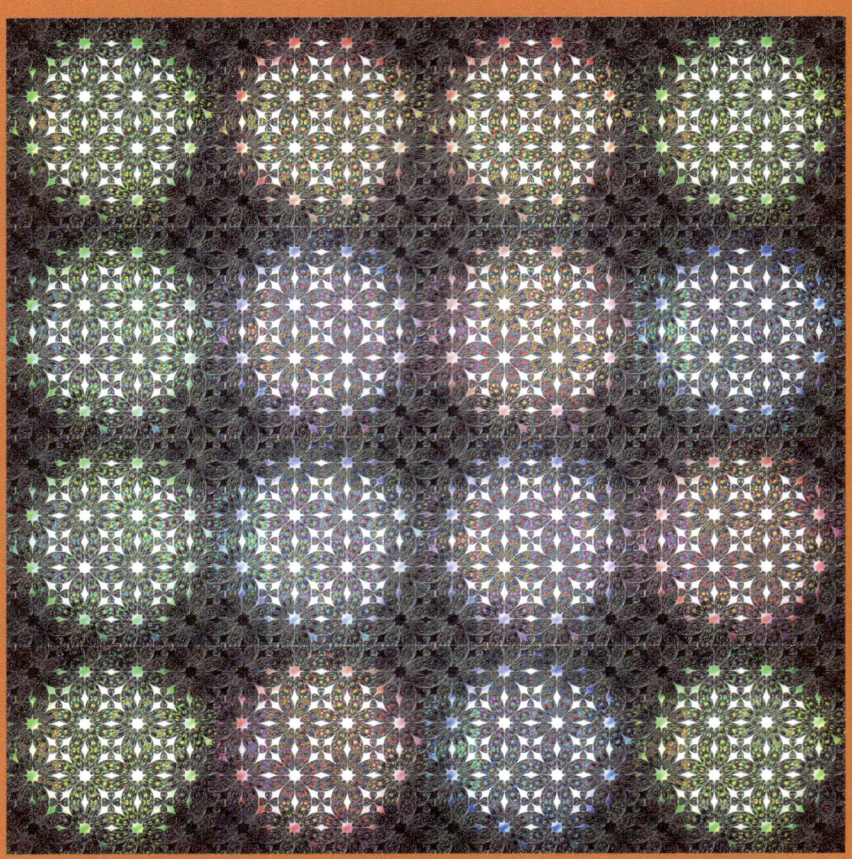

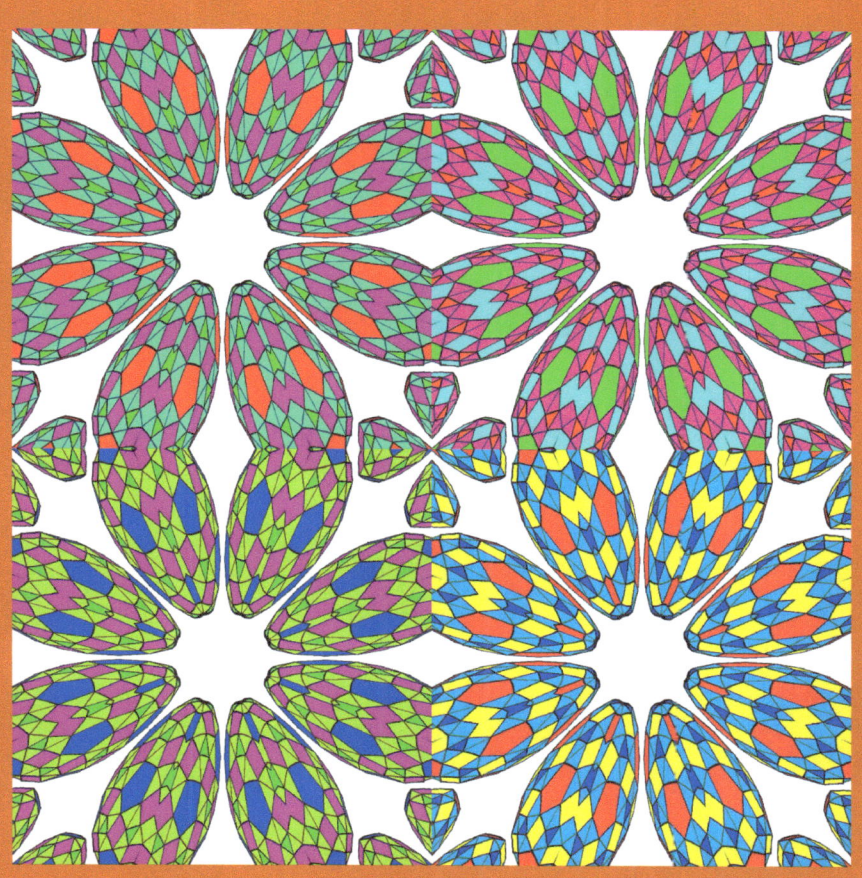

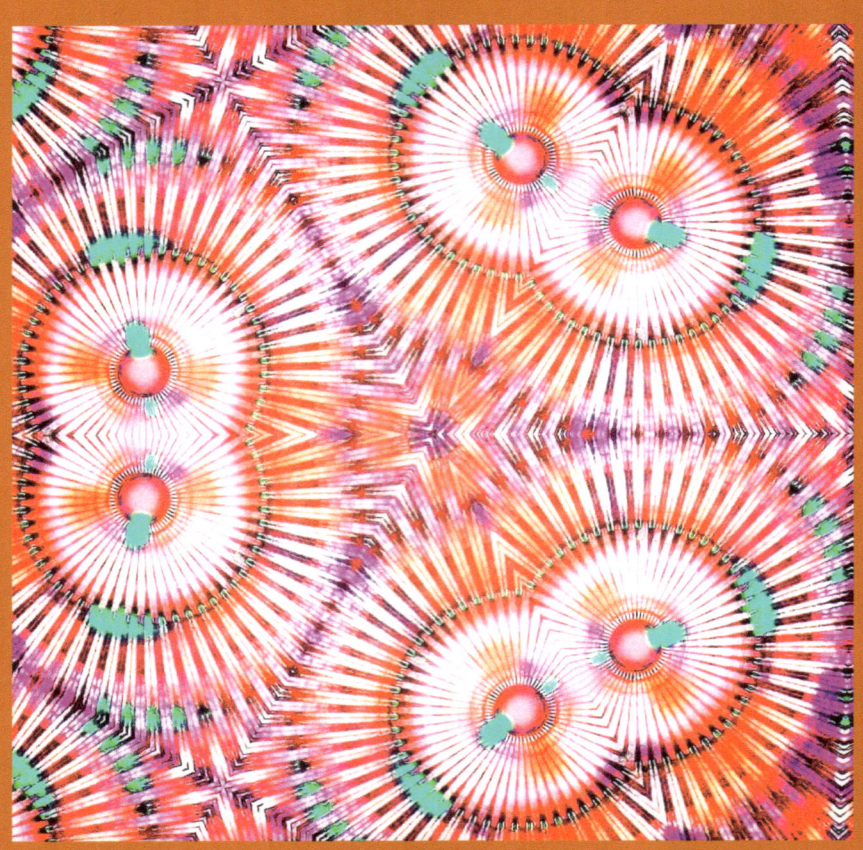

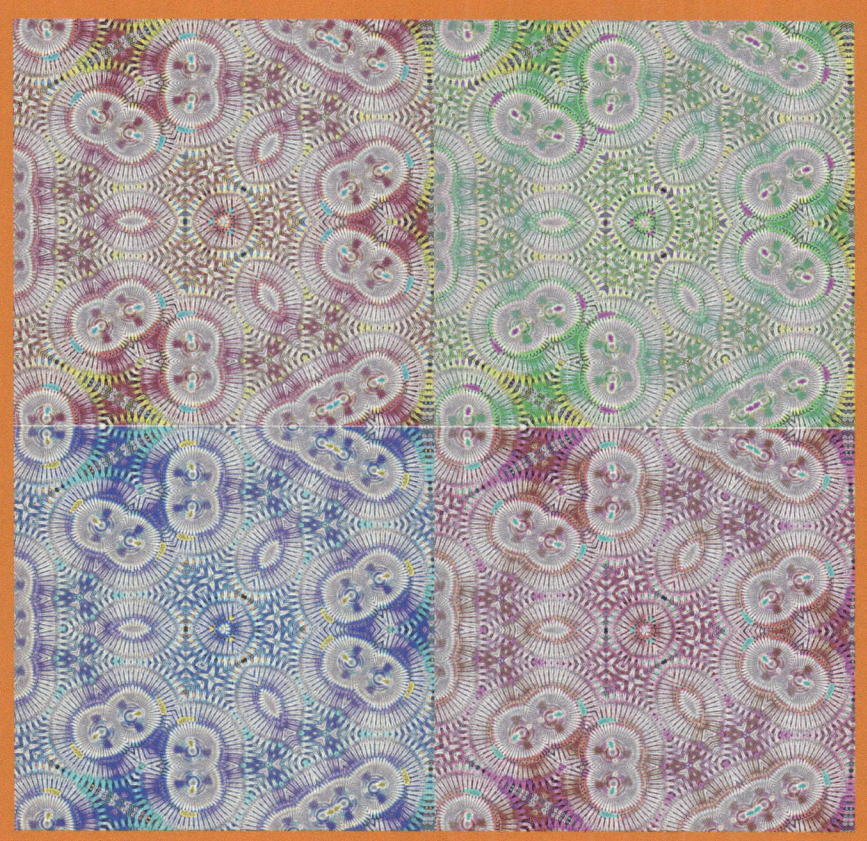

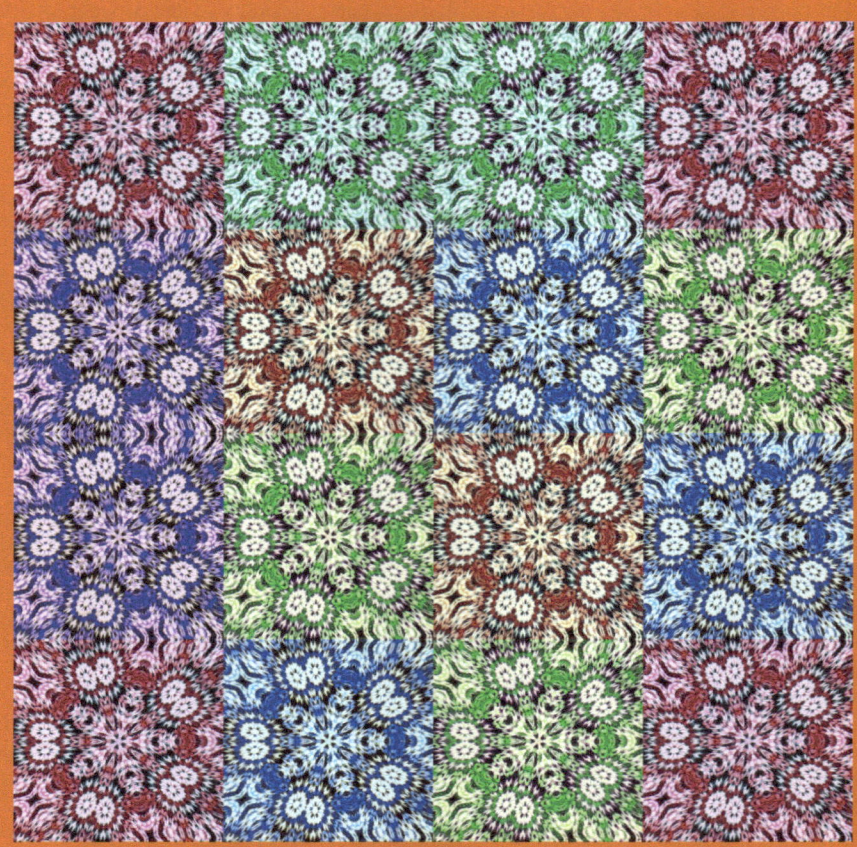

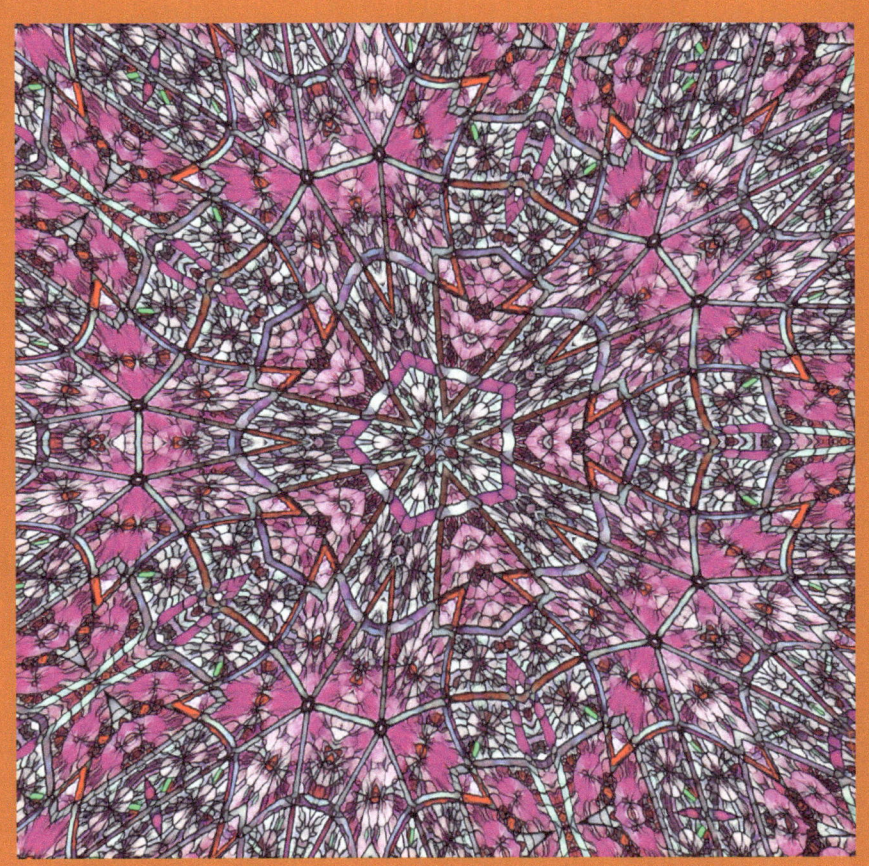

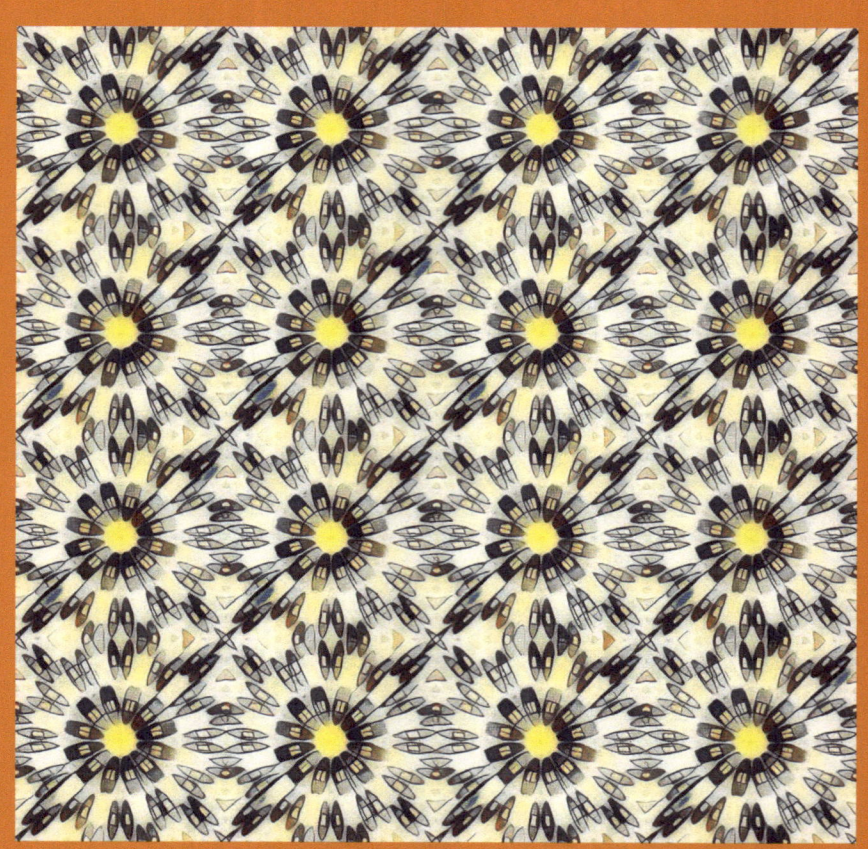

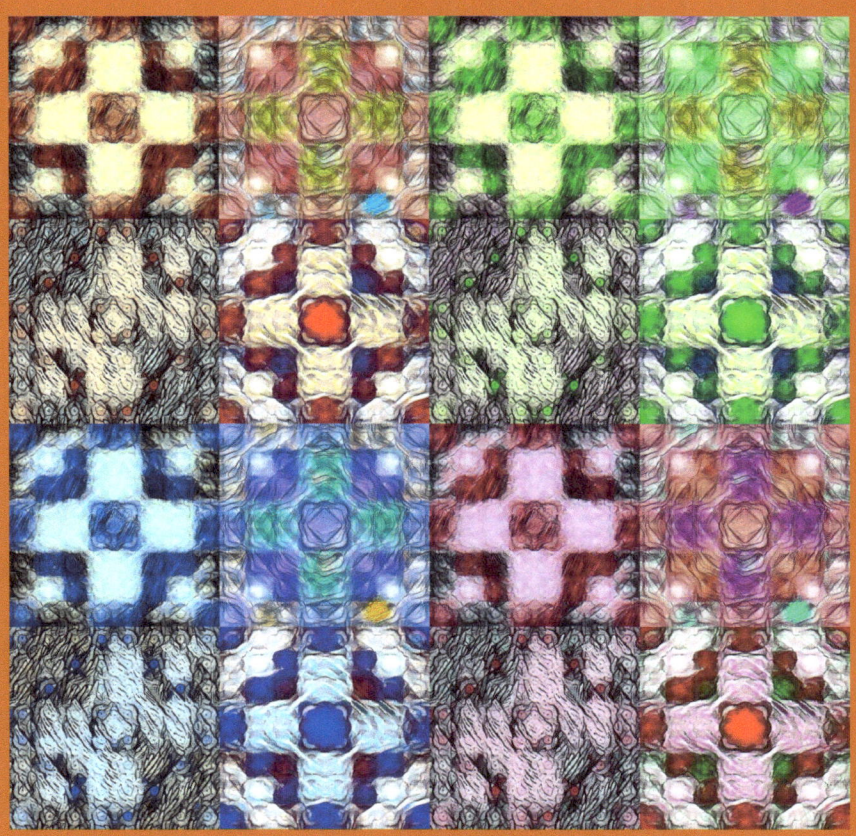

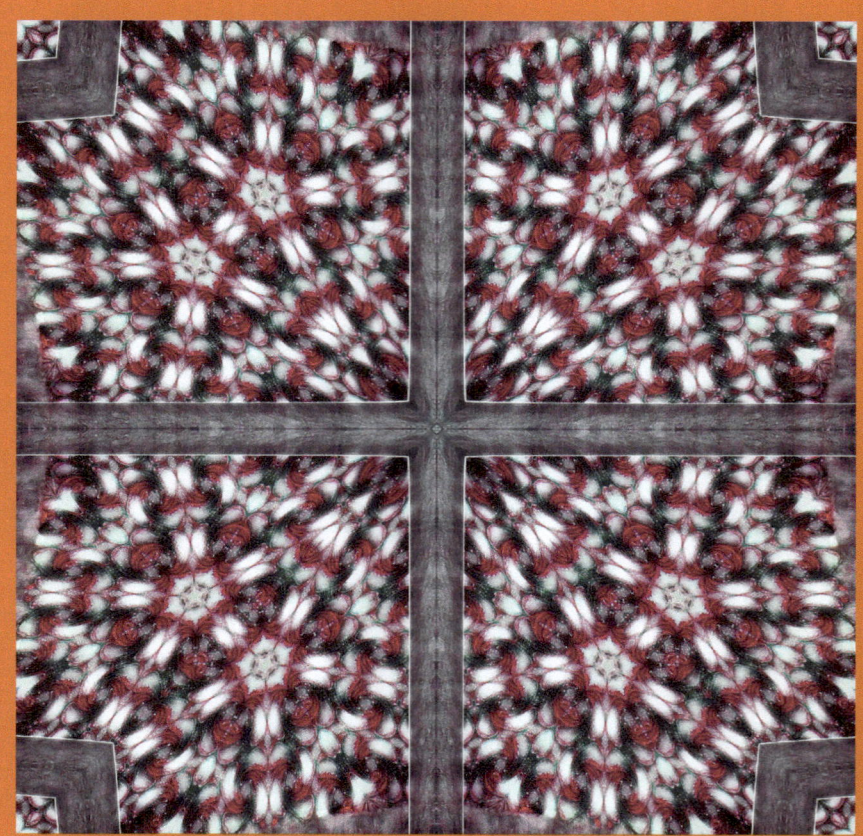

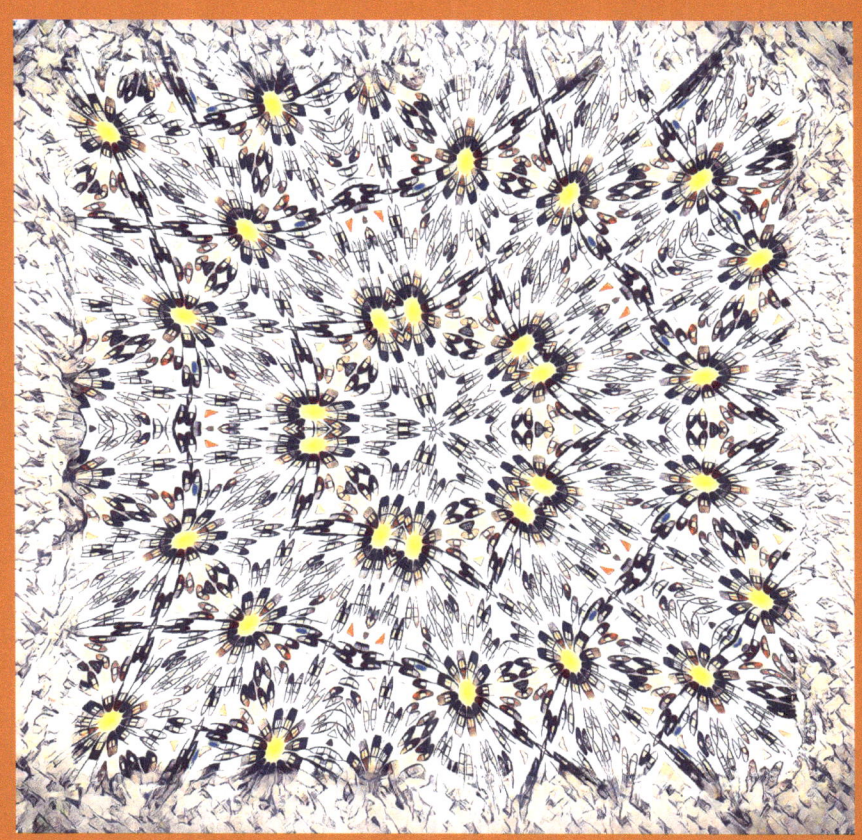

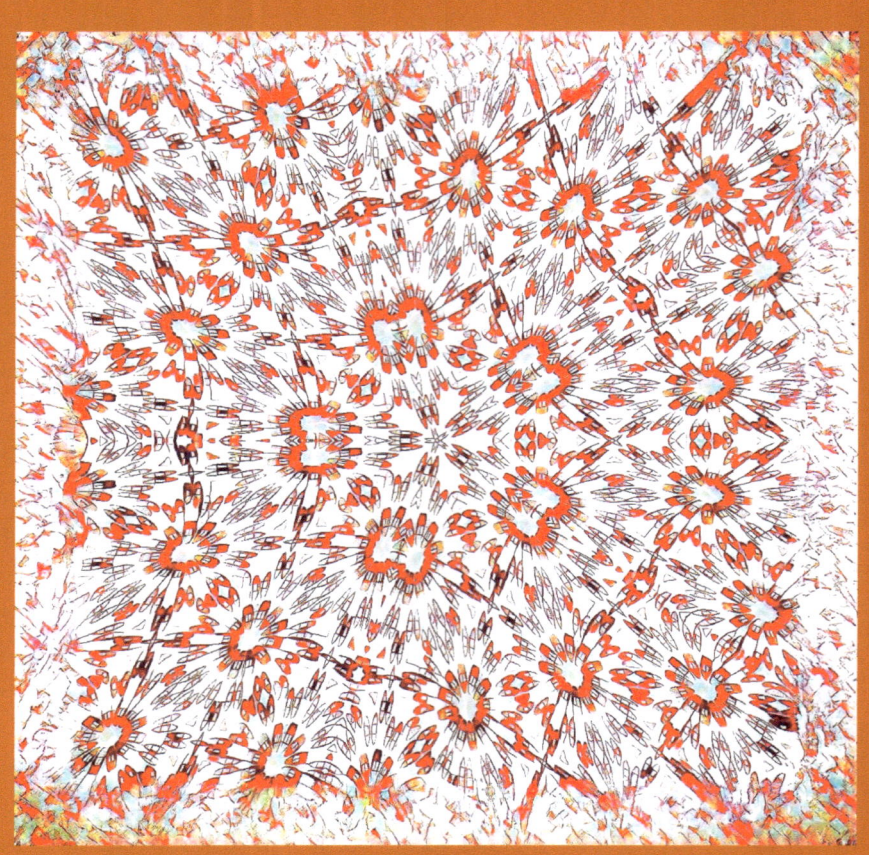

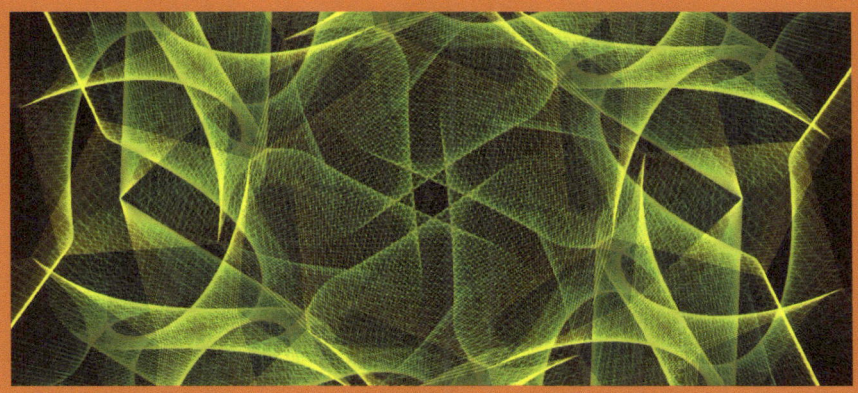

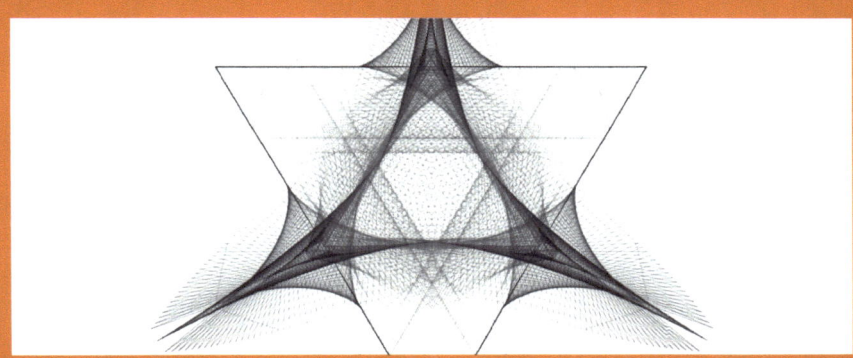

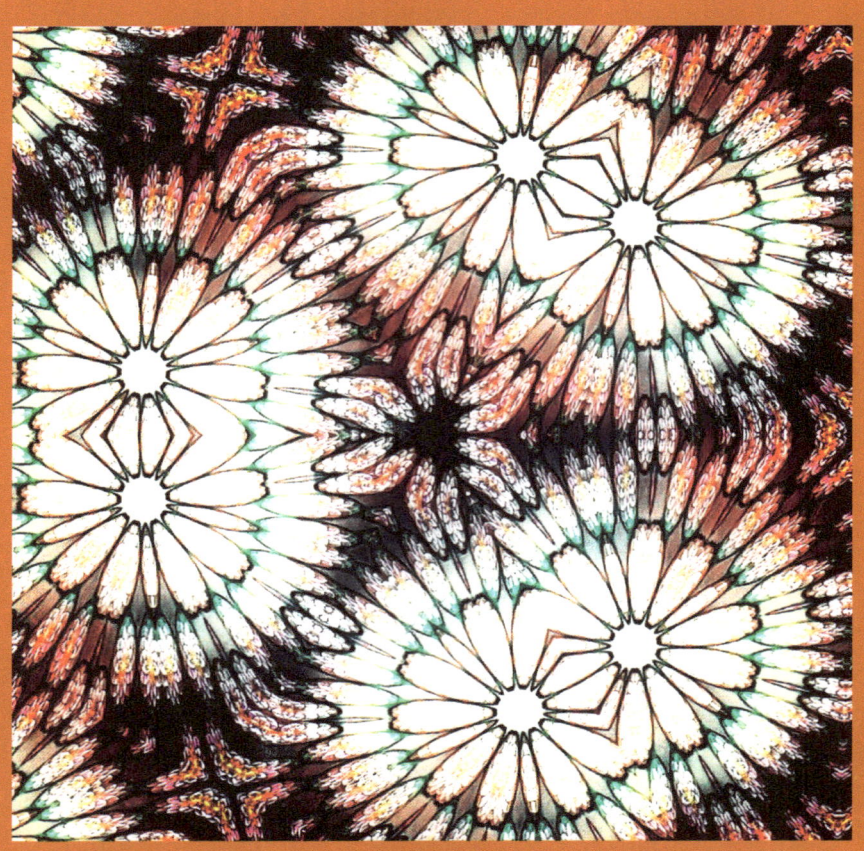

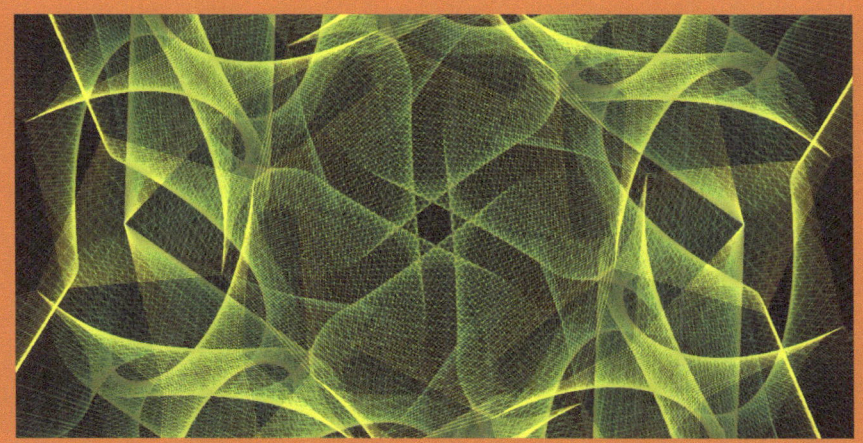

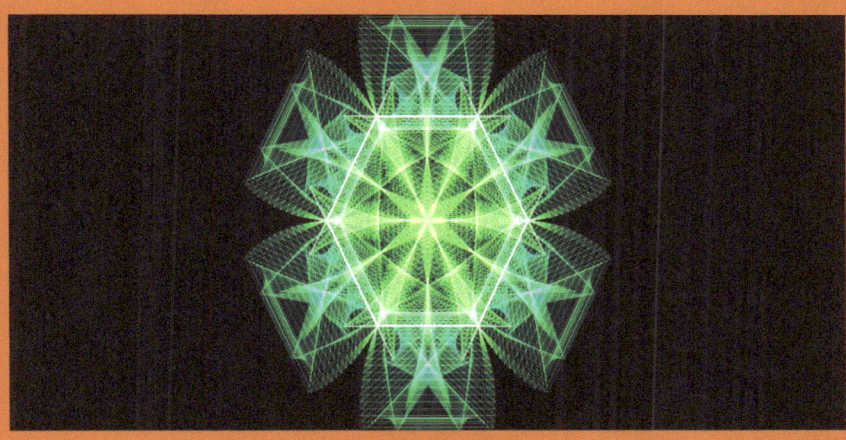

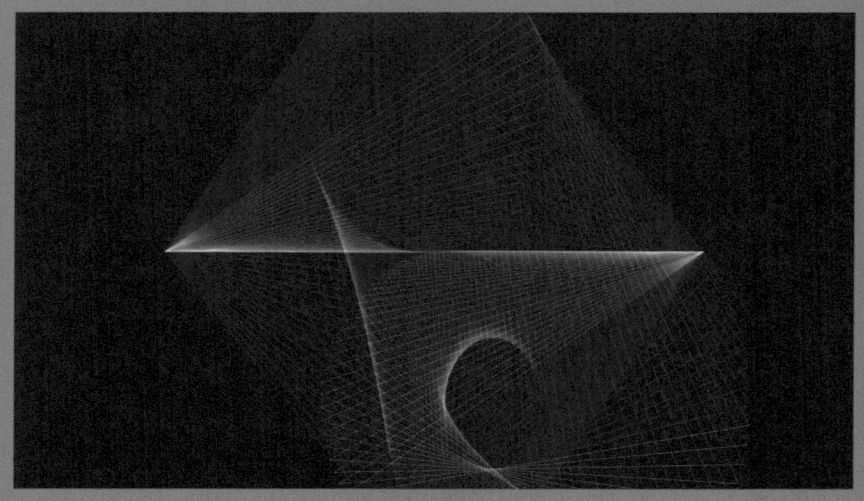

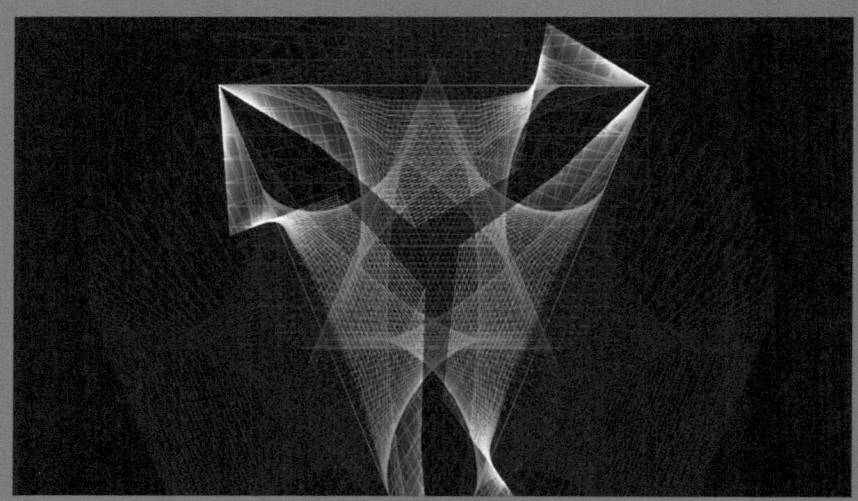

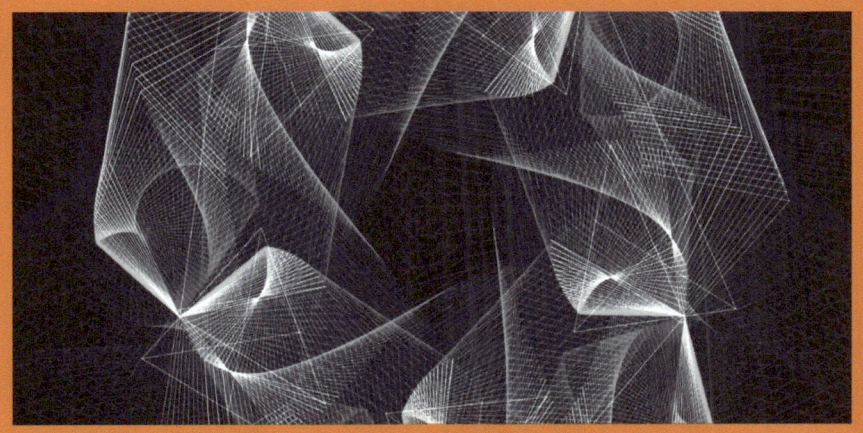

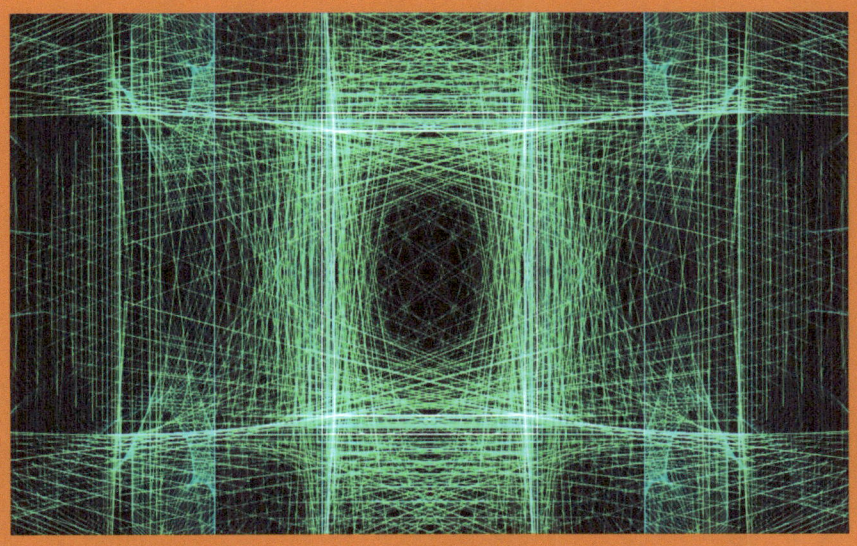

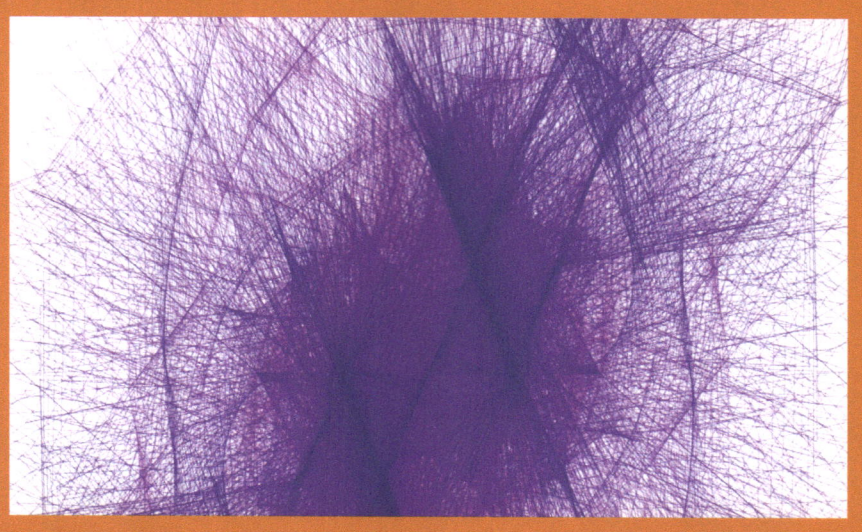

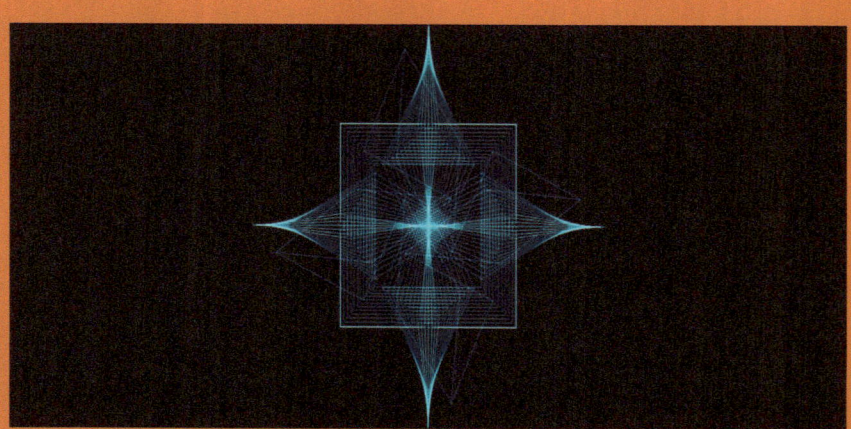

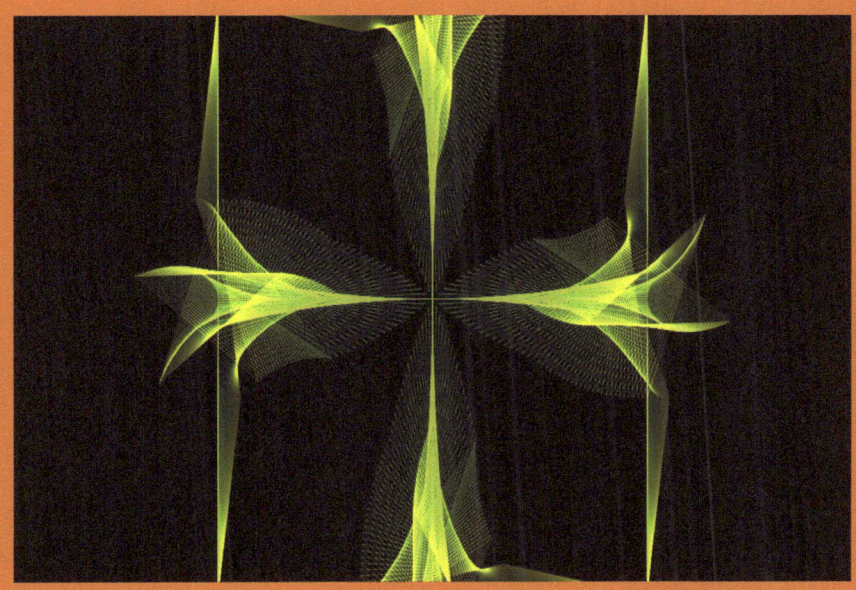

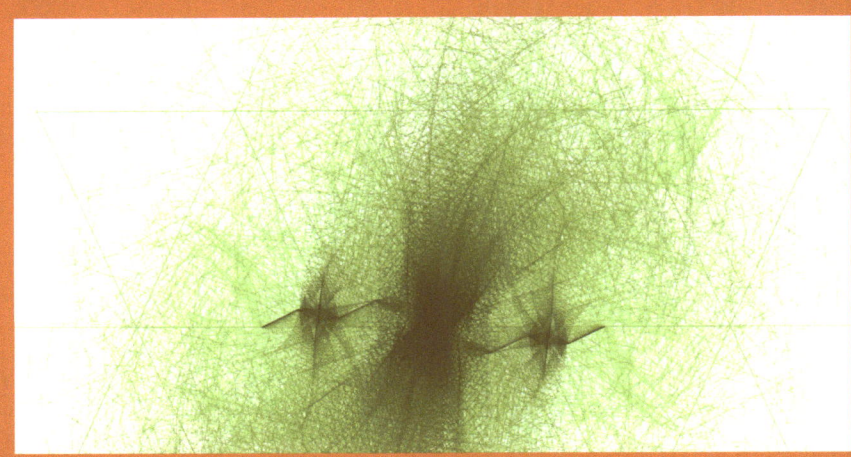

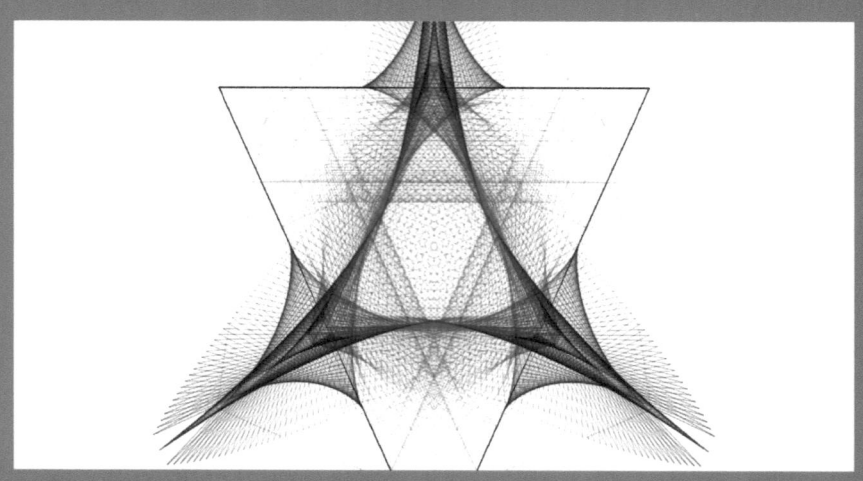

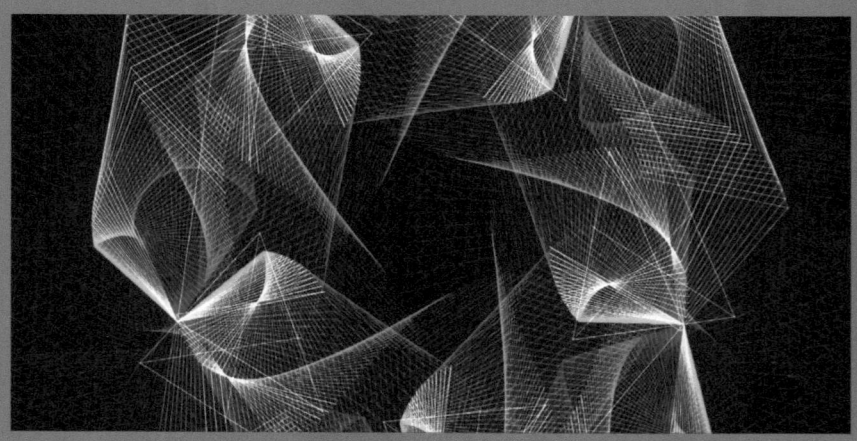

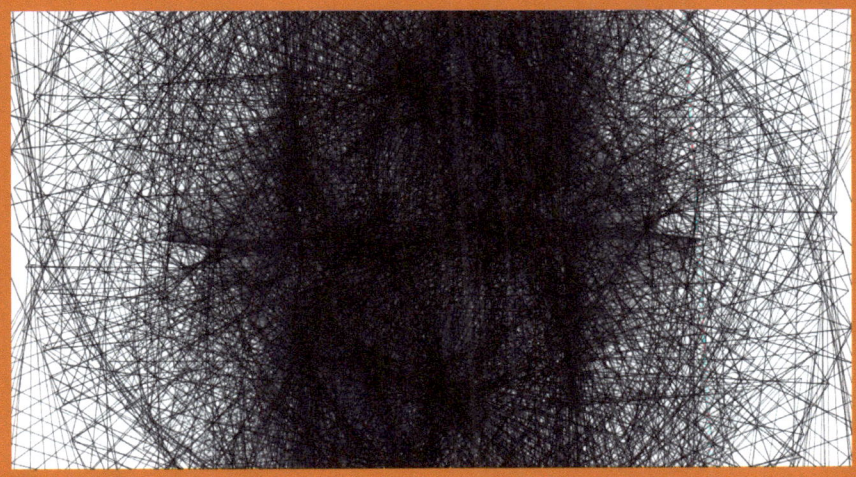

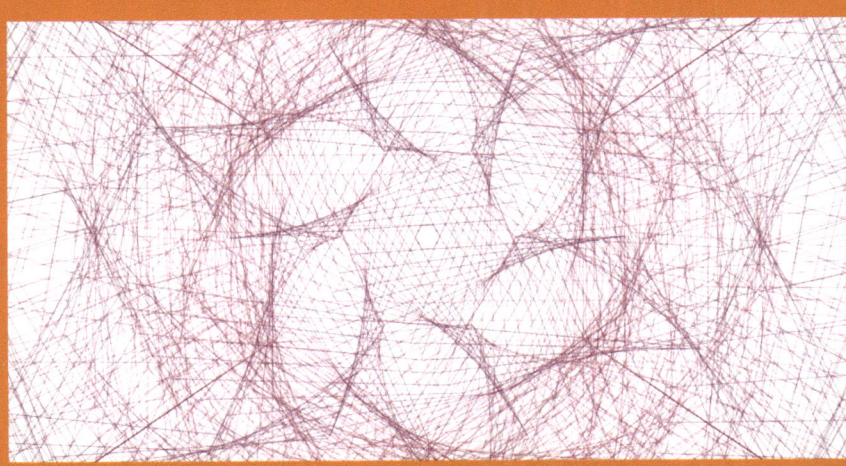

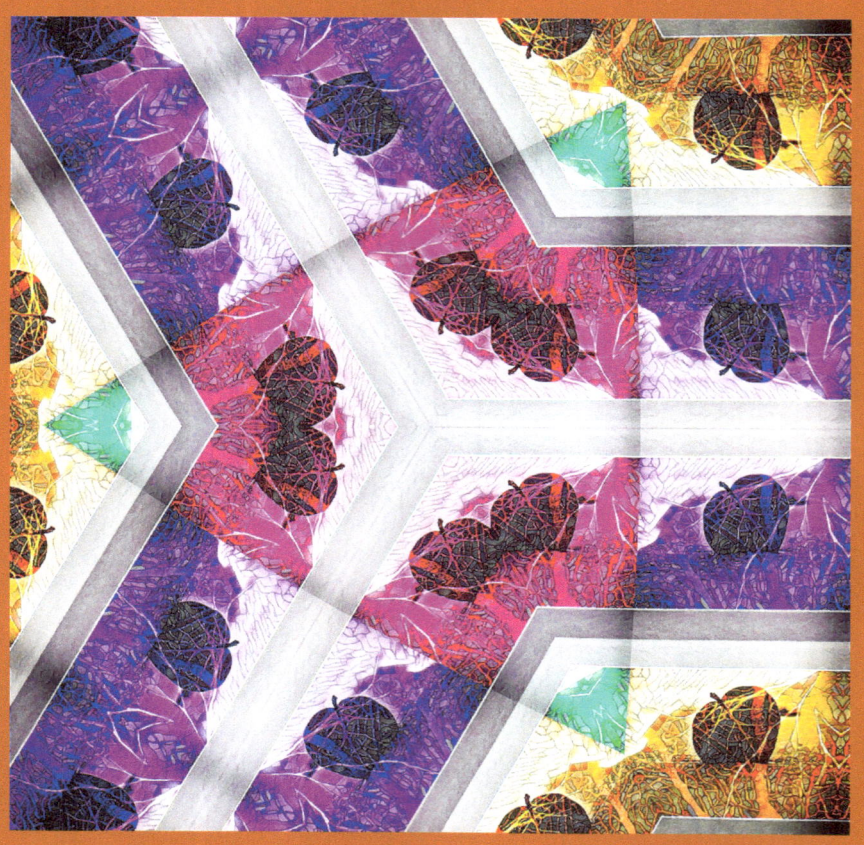

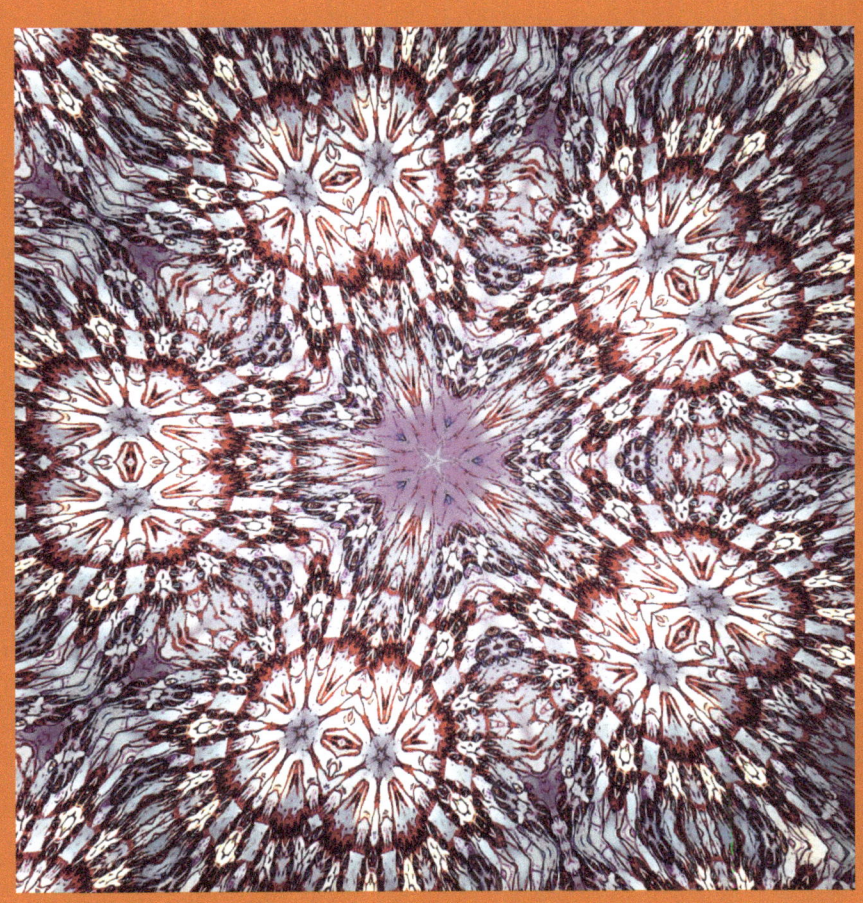

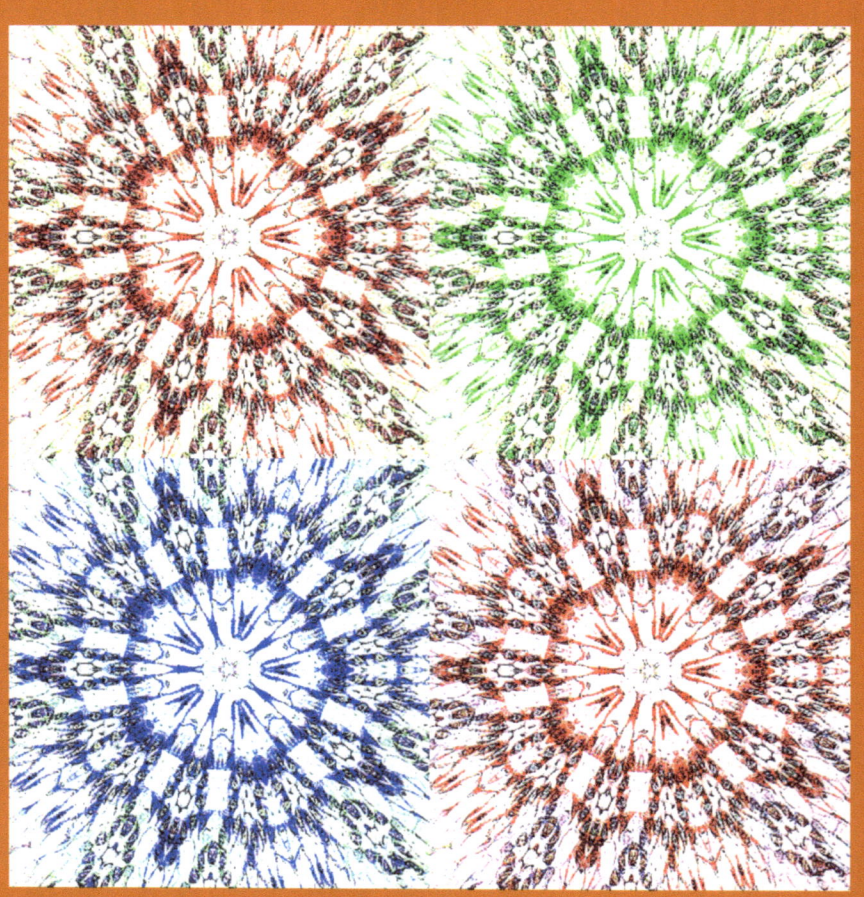

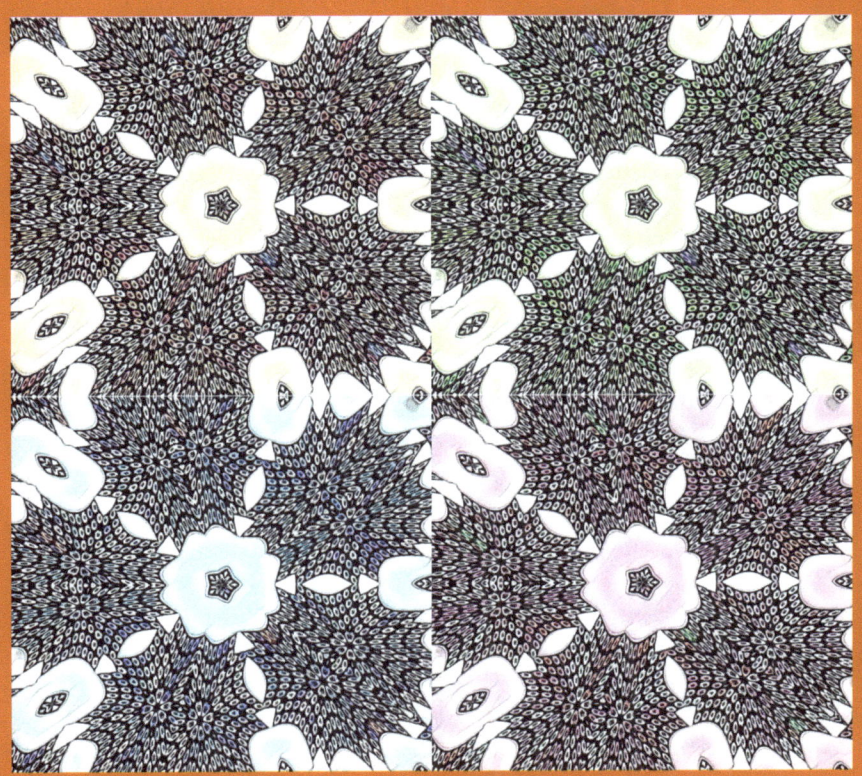

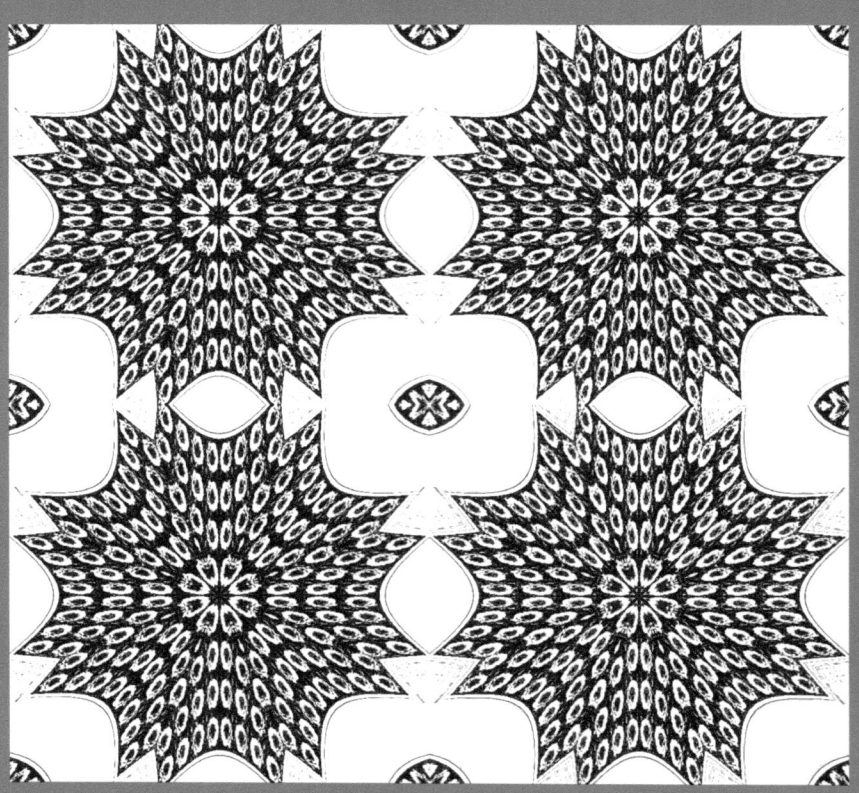

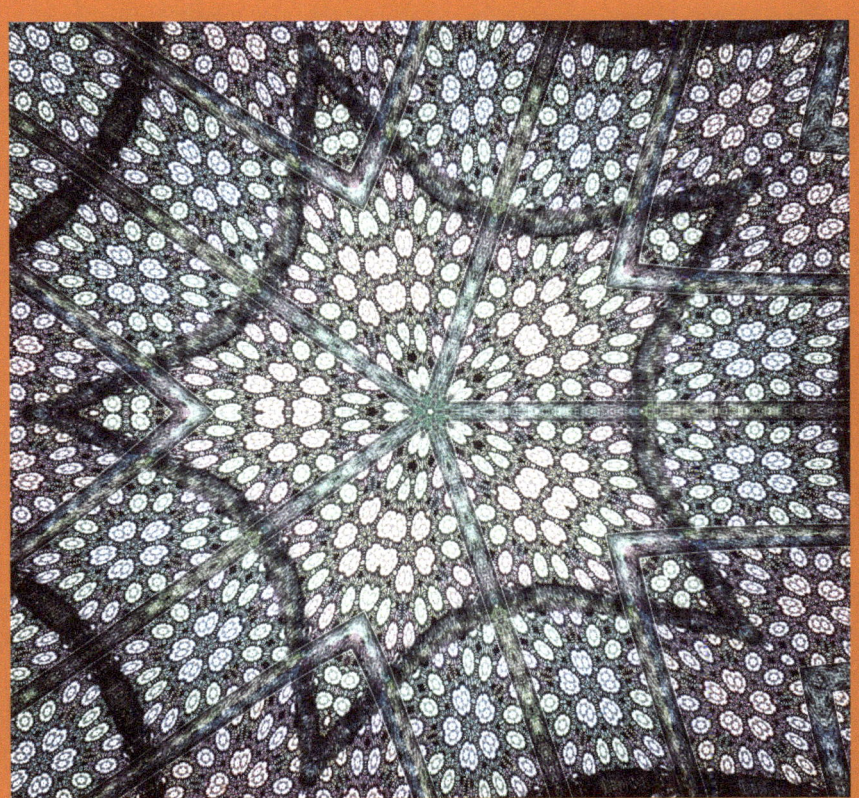

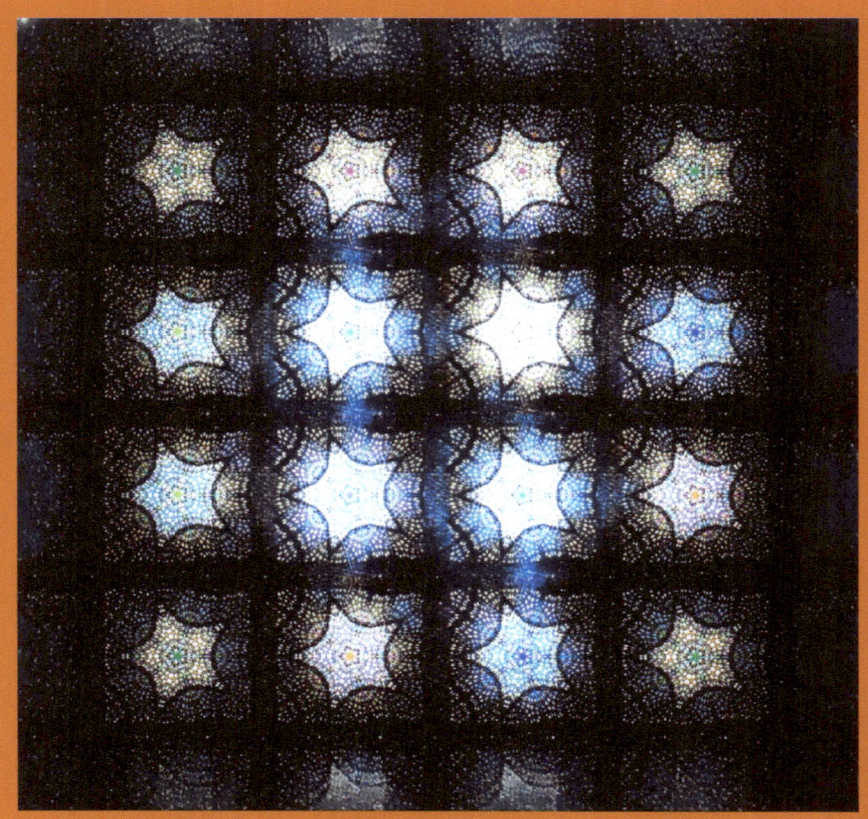

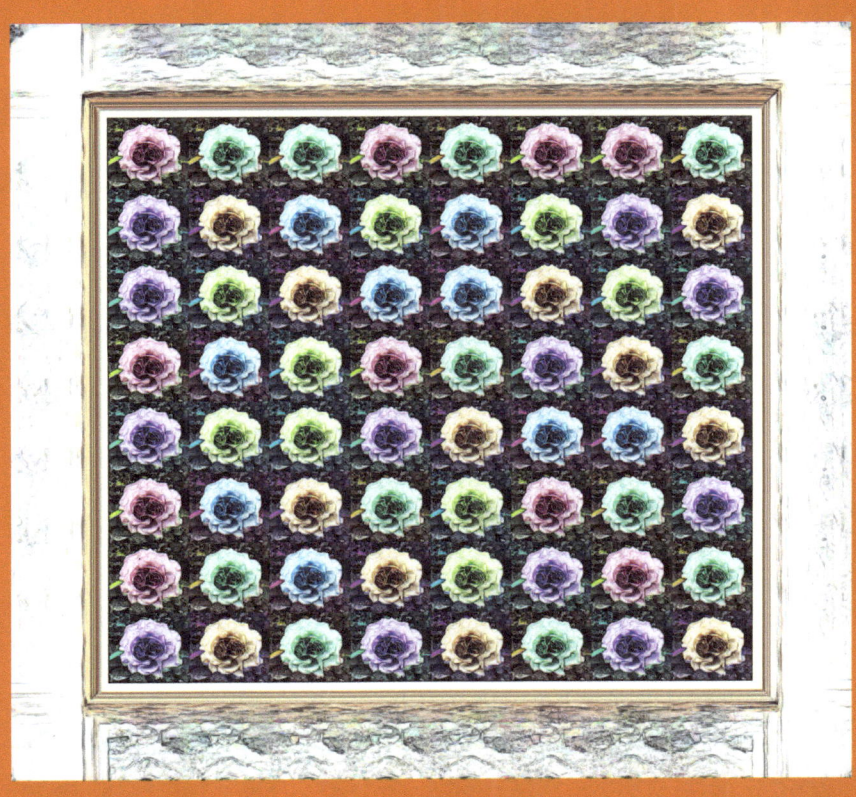

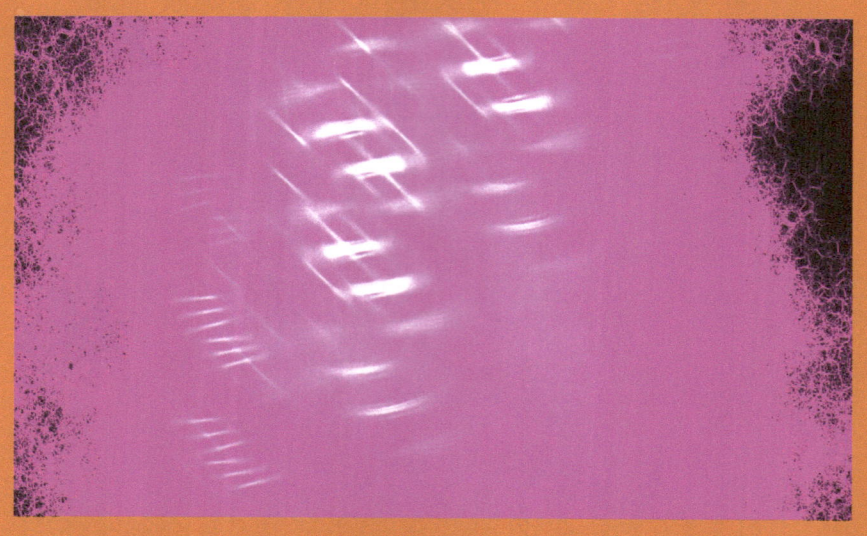

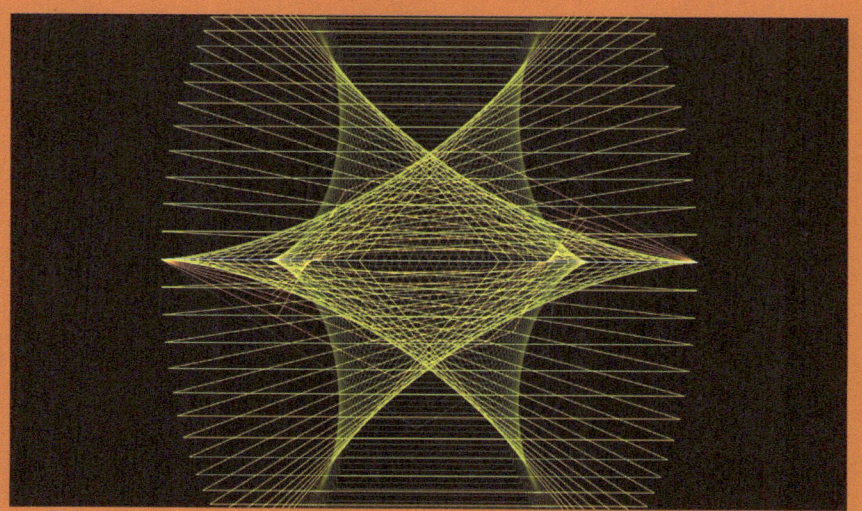

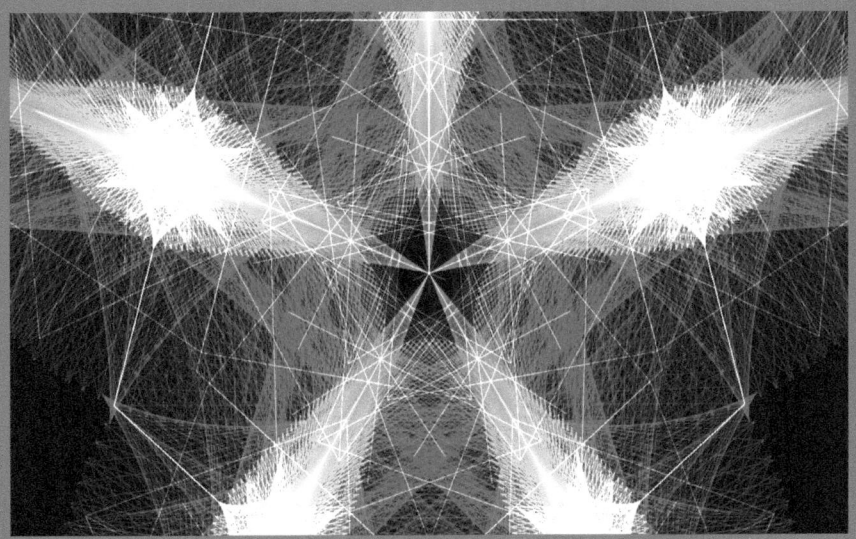

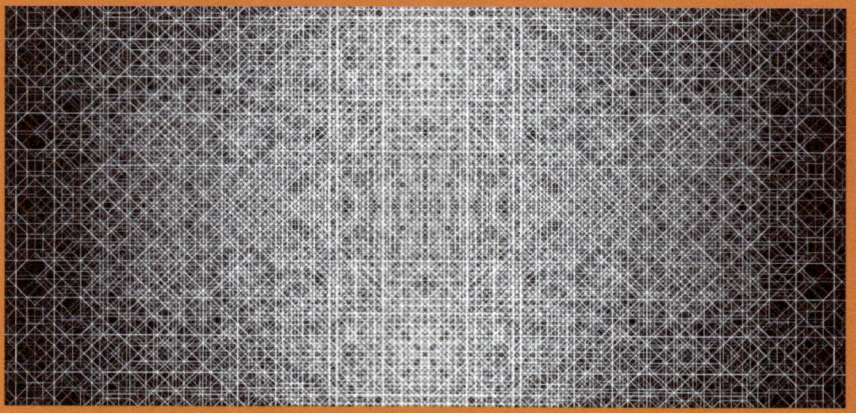

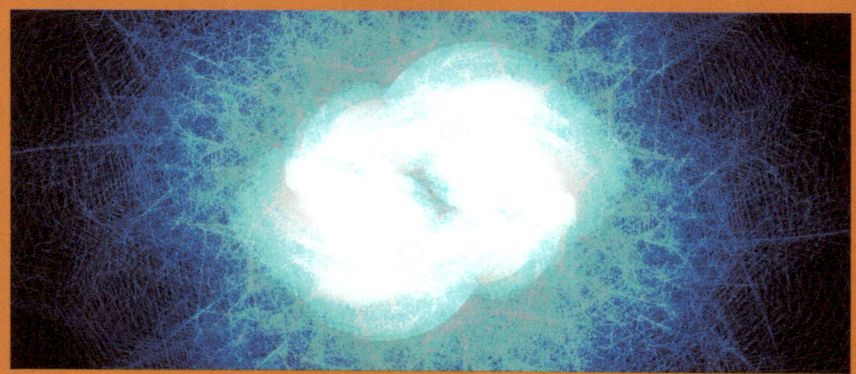

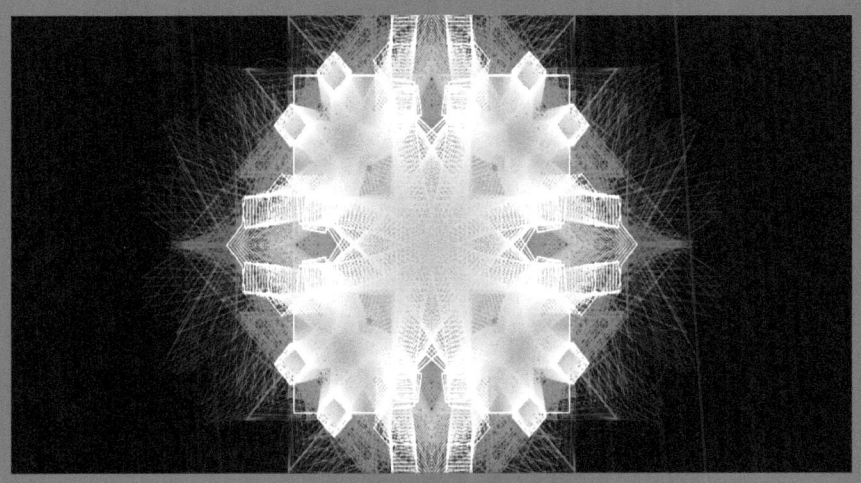

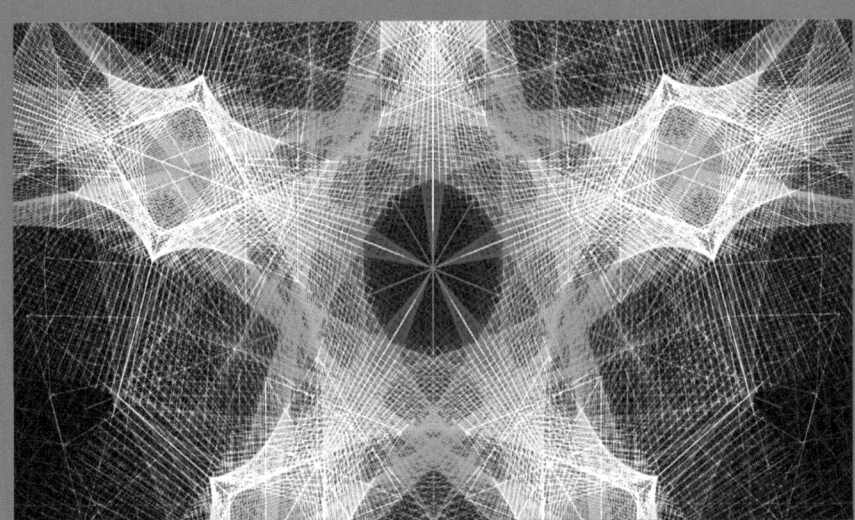

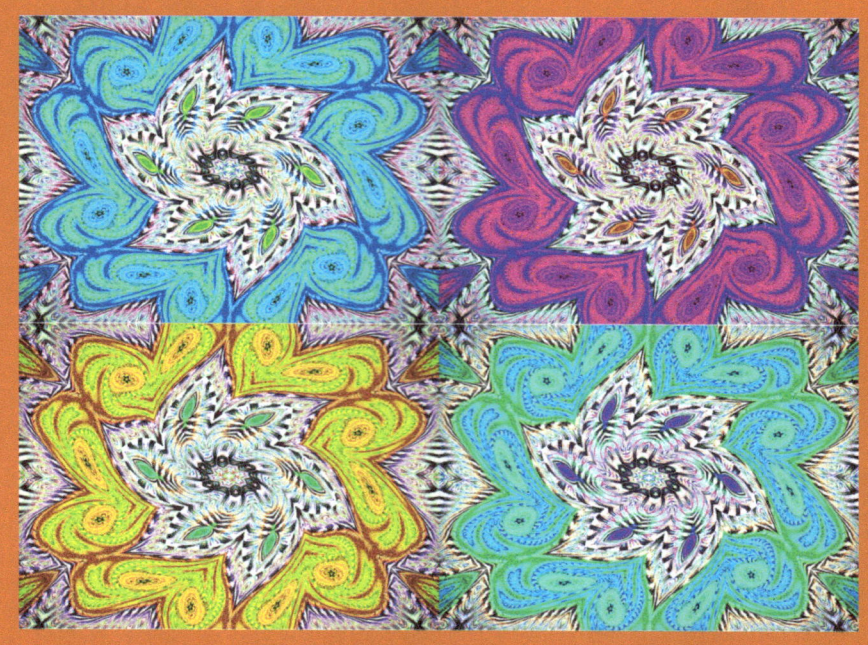

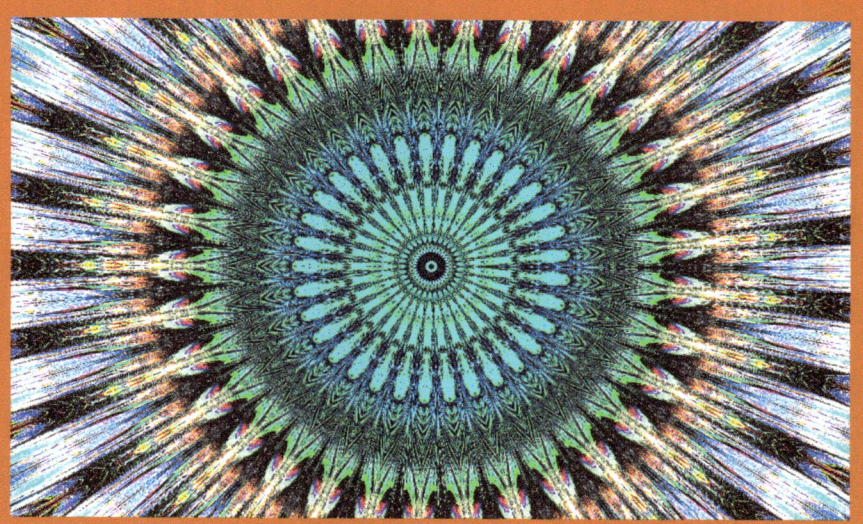

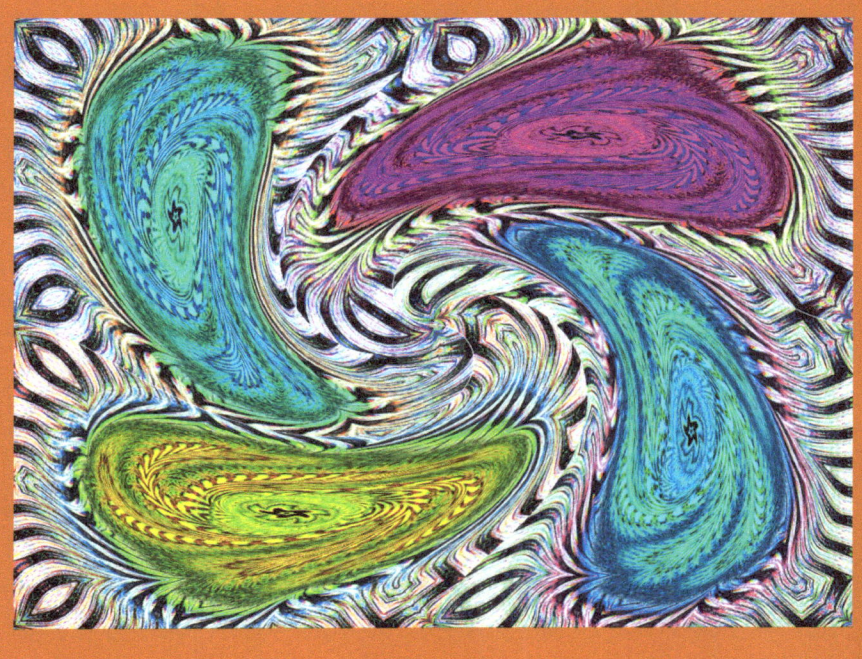

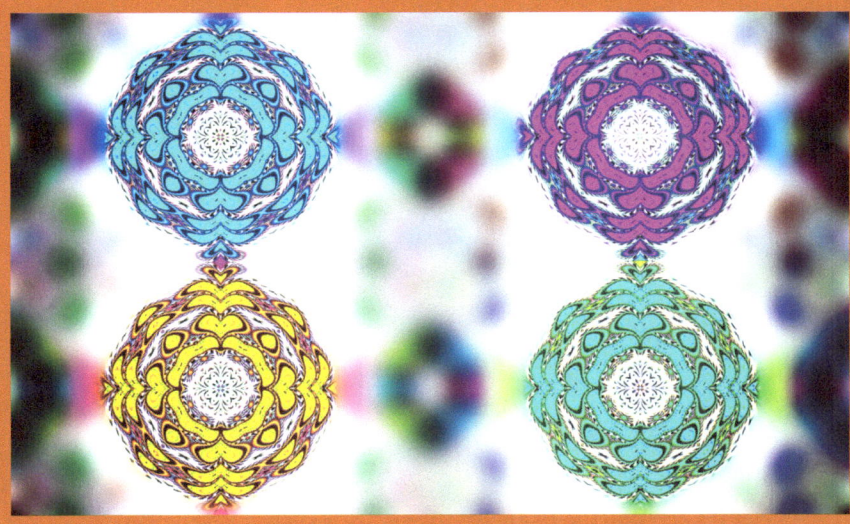

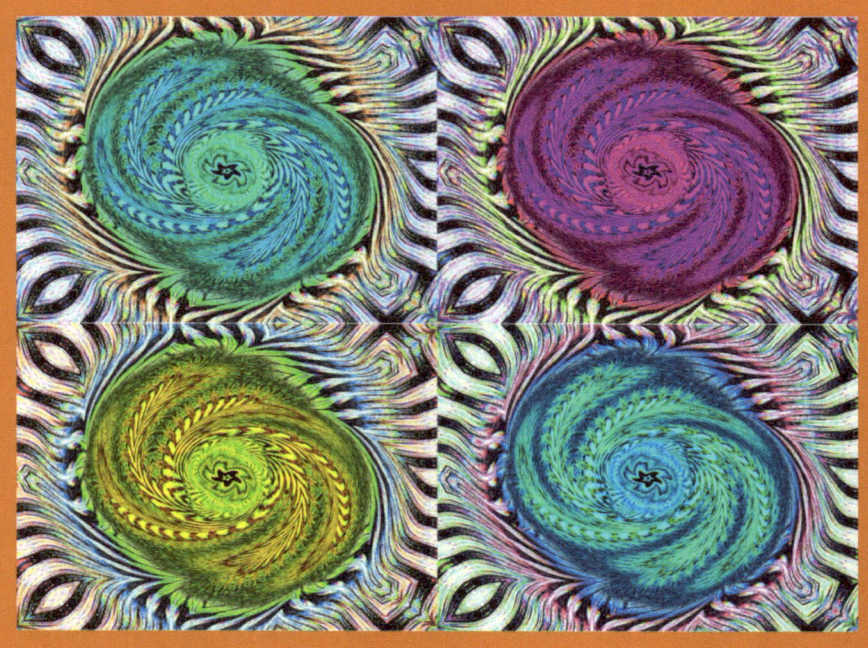

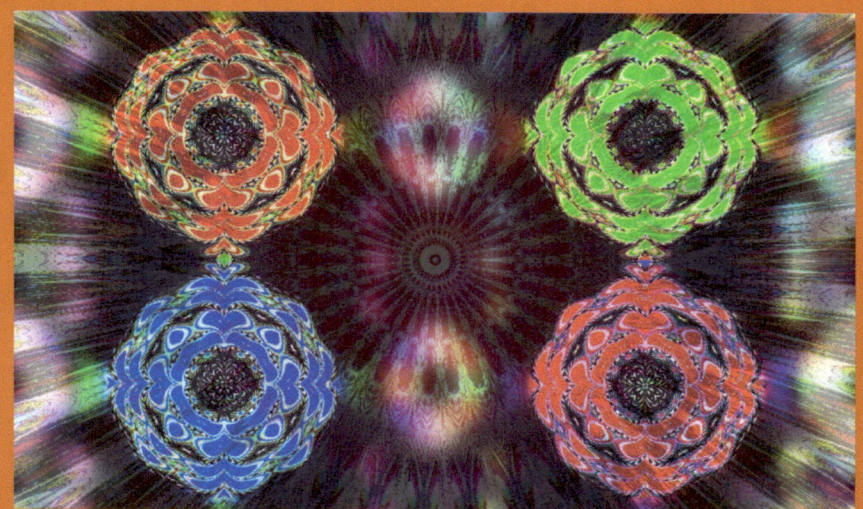

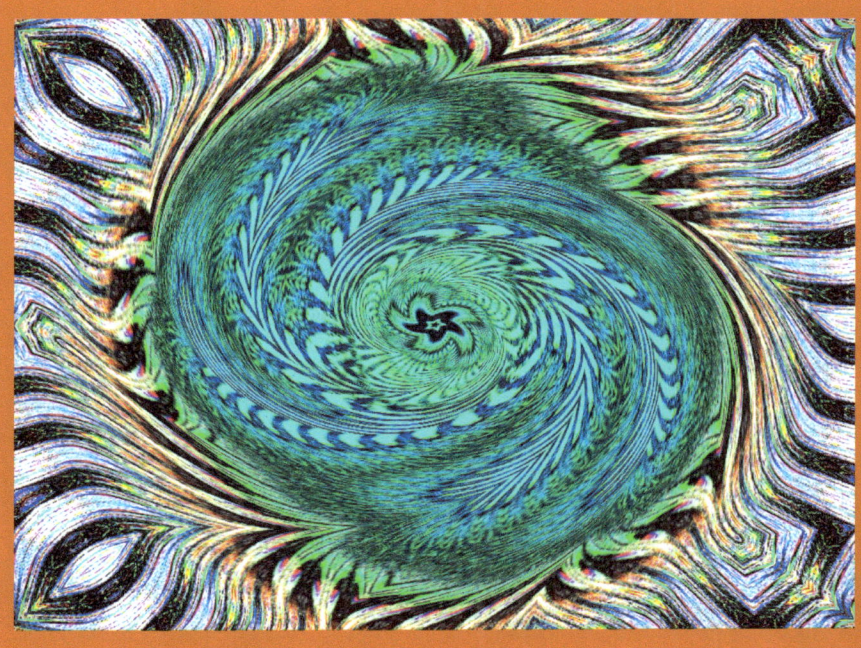

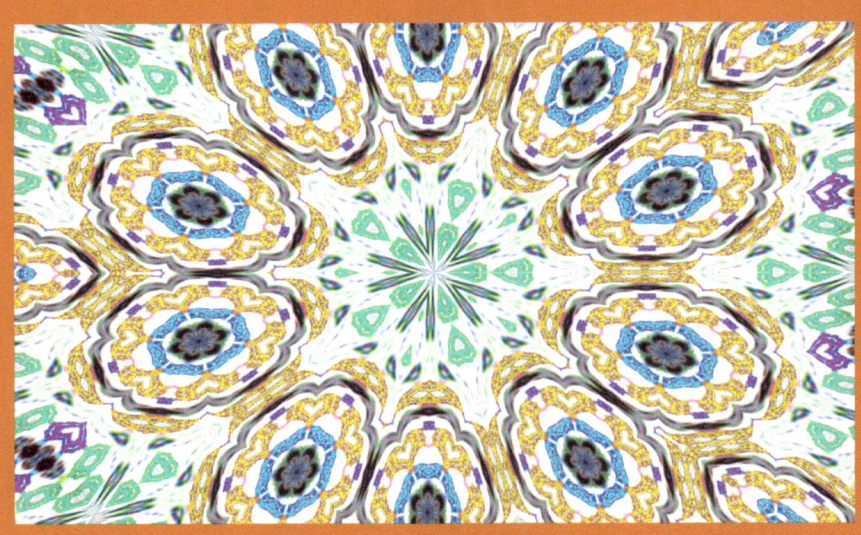

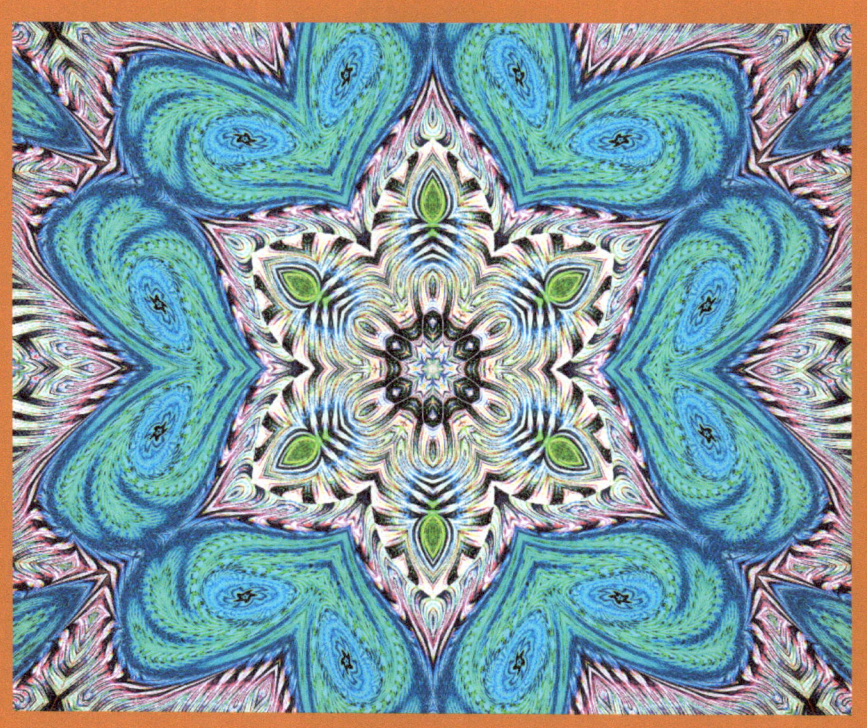

Best Regards,

Mary Kei

~~

Artist - Writer - Explorer

Corriculum vitae

CV

- Has studied for two years at the School of Journalism Laboratory.

- Has attended history and philosophy classes at Deree American College.

- Has attended drama art classes as a listener at the Veaki Drama School.

- Has dealt with photography and has been awarded in the magazine

"Photographer" in Greece, also is proposed in international exhibitions.

- Has written poetry and literature and poetry and has been awarded in a

Panhellenic competition.

- Has attended sculpture classes and has worked as a sculptor.

- Has attended a screenwriting seminar from the screenwriters

greek association, seminar of social media and of ancient greek

philosophy in Athens.

- Is involved in music composition and painting.

- Recently is active in the field of business as a freelancer

in buying and selling.